ROOSTER

ROOSTER

THE LIFE AND TIMES OF THE REAL ROOSTER COGBURN, THE MAN WHO INSPIRED TRUE GRIT

BRETT COGBURN

KENSINGTON BOOKS
www.kensingtonbooks.com

KENSINGTON BOOKS are published by

Kensington Publishing Corp.
119 West 40th Street
New York, NY 10018

All Kensington titles, imprints, and distributed lines are available at special quantity discounts for bulk purchases for sales promotion, premiums, fund-raising, and educational or institutional use.

Special book excerpts or customized printings can also be created to fit specific needs. For details, write or phone the office of the Kensington Special Sales Manager: Kensington Publishing Corp., 119 West 40th Street, New York, NY 10018. Attn. Special Sales Department. Phone: 1-800-221-2647.

Kensington and the K logo Reg. U.S. Pat. & TM Off.

ISBN-13: 978-0-7582-7494-6
ISBN-10: 0-7582-7494-7

First Kensington Trade Paperback Printing: September 2012
10 9 8 7 6 5 4 3 2

Printed in the United States of America

Contents

Introduction

In 1968, a Western novel called *True Grit* was published and became an instant classic. John Wayne's performance in the 1969 movie adaptation won him an Academy Award for his portrayal of the drunken, scruffy, one-eyed Deputy U.S. Marshal Rooster Cogburn. That character and Charles Portis's wonderful novel still resonate with audiences so much that the 2010 remake of *True Grit* was a box-office hit. Nowhere was the impact of the first movie stronger than among the many Cogburns scattered across the United States, especially in the backwoods areas that are our roots.

There are years and years of poor pioneer living behind many who bear the Cogburn name. Many of the descendants of my particular branch of the Cogburns still haunt the mountain hollows and river bottoms of western Arkansas and southeastern Oklahoma, as far from fame and fortune as people can get. At times, the Cogburn name has been a hard one in that neck of the woods, and bearing that moniker leads folks to assume you are one kind of an outlaw or another.

More than one Cogburn has taken a little hidden pride in the fact that Portis's character bore their last name. Even for those who never read the novel, John Wayne is a red, white, and blue icon. For those of us weaned on Fourth of July flag waving, the image of him as that lovable rogue with a patch over his eye dealing out justice to the bad guys with a gun in each fist is the epitome of manly virtue. Many a Cogburn boy since then has been given the nickname "Rooster." The name is so recognizable that the first question on a stranger's lips is often the same. Inevitably, they ask, "You mean like Rooster Cogburn?" It is no wonder that hints and folktales began to surface among the family of a real Rooster Cogburn almost simultaneously with the release of the first movie.

My Papaw used to say that if he had a nickel for every lie told to him that was sworn to be the truth, he would have been a rich man. If I had a nickel for every Cogburn who had a man in their family tree who was supposedly Portis's inspiration for Rooster Cogburn, I'd have managed a profit myself. I might not be rich, but I'd take Mama and the kids out for a Sunday T-bone and lobster tail. Despite the many claims I have heard of a real Rooster—some of which went so far as to claim that Charles Portis had visited with various family members to gain the basis for his character—I never for a second believed that Rooster Cogburn was anything but fiction.

My grandparents had survived the Depression and were of a generation that kept their skeletons in the closet. Somewhere in those years of my youth I learned that my great-grandfather, John Franklin Cogburn, had served time in the penitentiary. Supposedly, some of his kin had killed a revenuer back in the old days. During the trial, he was found in contempt of court for smart-aleck remarks to the judge and was given a year in the hoosegow. Getting that much information from my grandfather was like pulling teeth, and the only other thing I could gather was that John Franklin was a preacher in his later years, and so fine a man that he must have walked on rose petals with the smell of perfume on the air around him. I don't even know if my grandfather knew the whole story, as his father had died when he was very young. For many years I went about my life with little knowledge of my great-grandfather other than a few intriguing bits and pieces that didn't always match the man my Papaw had described.

And then, in the mid nineties, I met a distant cousin at a horse sale who offered a document that was to set me on a long and winding trail. Some days after the sale, the man mailed me a Xeroxed copy of a stained and tattered letter and envelope dated 1881. My recently met benefactor was certain that a real Rooster Cogburn had once existed, and his letter seemed to prove his point. The body of that letter stated that my great-grandfather was known as "Rooster" in the old days, and hinted at a hell of a story.

Many people develop the genealogy urge later in life, but this tantalizing clue absorbed me. I began to recall tiny snatches of mystery related to me over the years by ancient family members and set out to prove to myself once and for all whether there was a real Rooster Cogburn, and if he was indeed my great-grandfather. I happened to meet the noted Old West historian and author Glenn Shirley shortly after receiving the letter. He added fuel to my fire by hinting that my family name had some interesting stories behind it and suggested that I might be well served to look in the Fort Smith newspapers of the 1880s. Fifteen years later, after off-again and on-again research, I had satisfied my curiosity and shocked my pessimism. The tale I had gleaned from the old-timers of my youth, dug from dusty files, and pulled reluctantly from countless hours of staring at newspaper microfilm was stranger by far than fiction.

The work that follows is the story of John Franklin Cogburn, born in the wake of the Civil War and a young man during the lawless, wild days of Hanging Judge Parker's court. In no way, shape, or form do I attempt to take credit from Charles Portis for his novel *True Grit*. That plot was solely of his making and the fruit of his talent and imagination. While his Rooster

Cogburn bears some resemblances to the actual man, it doesn't lead me to believe that Portis's character was anything more than the result of his talent, a feel for the time and place, and solid research on western Arkansas and Indian Territory during Judge Isaac Parker's time on the bench at Fort Smith. Portis was himself from southern Arkansas, a newspaper man, and he knew how to get the "flavor" right. I do assert that there was a real-life, honest-to-goodness Rooster Cogburn, and his battle with Parker's court and Deputy U.S. Marshals is a worthy tale in its own right. I present a list of curious correlations and names from John Franklin's life that correspond to *True Grit*. Perhaps Portis was aware of John Franklin's story, but I can only speculate and present the facts. Portis has long since stated that Rooster was a composite or a collage of many men and marshals of the era, and I don't doubt that is true.

Every major assertion in this work is backed by solid research. Where folklore is relied upon it is duly qualified as such, and those unproven portions are not crucial to the major points and facts of the biography. Also, Franklin Cogburn's story couldn't be told without referencing other events that took place during the old days of Judge Parker's court at Fort Smith. I have endeavored to present some unique and original research bits about the outlaws and lawmen of the era, as much for flavor and effect as for historical scholarship. I hope this little book will give the reader a tiny window into the time and place. Back in the wild and woolly days of yore there was a real Rooster Cogburn, and he was my great-grandfather. But then again, it's his story and not mine. . . .

1

Blood Feud

Black Springs wasn't much of a town as towns went, even in the backwoods of Arkansas. It might have been more aptly termed a "spot in the road," as some folks will say, more of a community than a town proper. There was only one building that bore a second look and that was the general store. Even that wasn't much in the way of opulence, its weathered timbers grayed and lacking a single coat of paint. The store commanded the settlement more by height than by any pretentious display of architecture and beauty, being the only two-story structure in sight. The first floor consisted of the meager offerings of merchandise the poor folks who graced its dark interior might want or afford, and the upstairs served duty as the local Masonic lodge. The large front porch overlooked the hardscrabble log and sawmill lumber buildings scattered along a stretch of dusty road that led west through the mountains into Indian Territory. The mangy old hound lying at the foot of the porch and scratching a flea off its bony ribs was in perfect keeping with the pace and prosperity of the tiny settlement.

The cold wind blowing and the gray clouds sliding over the

pine treetops on the mountaintop above town reminded everyone that it was the dead of winter. Most folks were huddled around their fireplaces or standing over warmly ticking stoves, so not many saw the tall young man ride into town. He came up the trail from Fancy Hill on a pretty good horse for a hill boy. He left the animal out of the wind on the leeward side of the store and began to eke his way on foot from one building to the next.

Many in Black Springs would have known him, or at least recognized him for one of his clan. All of the men of his family were stamped much the same—high cheekbones, square chins, thick mustaches, and brown eyes that glittered like those of an Indian. The fact that he was bigger than most of his clan wasn't what gave pause to those who saw him on that morning. Every man in the mountains was a hunter in some form or fashion, and it was obvious that Franklin "Rooster" Cogburn was stalking somebody.

It wasn't unusual for a man to arrive in town with a rifle in his hands, as the roads could be dangerous to travel and leaving your shooter at home was a sure way to run short of meat in the cookpot. An armed man usually stored his gun to pick up later in whatever business or home he visited first if he came on foot, or he left it on his horse. Franklin didn't leave his Winchester anywhere. In fact, he carried it across his saddle when he arrived instead of having it in a scabbard, as if he were ready to jump shoot a deer or a turkey. And when he started down the street on foot, the gun was still in his hands.

Mountain folk can smell trouble just as easy as smoke on the wind, and the word rapidly spread throughout the settlement that Franklin was on the prowl. And word spread just as quickly who it was that he was hunting. Folks gave him room just like you did a mean old bull when you had to walk across your neighbor's pasture. Butting into somebody else's business was always chancy, much less antagonizing one of the Cogburns. There were too damned many of them to risk getting crossways with—not if a man valued his peace and wanted to stay out of a fight. It was best to let the Law handle the matter, and that was bound to happen, considering it was a Deputy U.S. Marshal that Franklin was looking for with blood in his eye.

Franklin made no attempt to hide the fact that he was looking for a fight with J. D. Trammell, and he quietly slandered the man's name to any who asked. He had heard Trammell was in town, and had ridden seven miles through the mountains to corner him. The rumor mill had it that Cogburns believed Trammell was working undercover either for the Revenue Service or for Judge Parker's court. Trammell had lived and worked for a while among the Cogburns in their stronghold at Fancy Hill, but had recently fled the community due to tension between him and some of the clan.

Lots of the citizens of Montgomery County made whiskey, and the Cogburns made more than anybody. The old Hanging Judge and his army of badge packers out of Fort Smith got a lot of press chasing train robbers and murderers in the Indian Territory, but people of the time knew that the marshals' main job was arresting whiskey peddlers and moonshiners. The Law was bound and determined to stem the distilling of illegal liquor, and especially to keep it out of the nearby Indian Territory. The mountain folks begrudgingly admired craftiness, and the "revenuers," as they often called the deputy marshals and other government men, could be especially sneaky in locating and busting up a man's stills. The kind of men brave enough or outlaw enough to break the law making whiskey often didn't look too kindly on anyone threatening their means of living, and a detective working undercover risked life and limb.

And there were other things that a Cogburn would tolerate even less than a revenuer. Many of the wives of the Cogburns and other families in the area claimed that Trammell was visiting their homes while their men were gone and using strong-arm tactics to force them to inform on who was making whiskey and where the stills were located. Always hotheaded and ready for a fight, Franklin had come to Black Springs to set things right. Nobody, and he meant *nobody*, was going to abuse the women of his family. A killing was in order.

J. D. Trammell was indeed a Deputy U.S. Marshal, but what Franklin didn't know was that Trammell wasn't in Black Springs. However, Montgomery County Sheriff G. W. Golden just happened to be in town on other business. The first thing he came across at a distance was Franklin armed, angry, and hunting a man whom Golden knew to be a fellow officer of the law. He immediately went to seek the help of the local constable, whose name has unfortunately been lost to history. Both lawmen were in agreement that Franklin should be disarmed, but neither of them was anxious to confront him.[1]

Among the people of southern Montgomery County, the twenty-two-year-old Franklin was known as an honest fellow, quick to lend his help, and a fine hand with a team of horses. While he may have been a likable sort, he was also known to be a part of the large moonshining operation run by some of the rougher sort in his family. He had a quick temper and would fight at the drop of a hat, and it was the opinion of more than a few citizens that his wild streak would eventually come to no good end.

Sheriff Golden knew that most of the Cogburns could be a little hard to handle when they were on the prod, but what most concerned him was the Winchester Franklin was carrying. In a country chock full of squirrel shooters, Franklin had a reputation as one of the finest marksmen in the mountains. Many of the mountain men were fond of whiskey and apt to resist a lawman when in their cups. Franklin wasn't drinking, but he was a Cogburn. They were notoriously ornery, and taking the gun away from him could be a little touchy if he didn't want to give it up.

The two lawmen were taking no chances they didn't have to, and they waited for Franklin outside the door of the store. When Franklin emerged, Sheriff Golden confronted him politely while the constable stepped in behind him with a drawn pistol. Heated words were exchanged, but they had the drop on Franklin and he eventually turned his weapon over to the sheriff.

Franklin made no apologies for hunting Deputy Marshal Trammell and readily admitted that he had come to kill him. Sheriff Golden knew that there would have been a fight had Trammell been in town, and he needed something to hold his prisoner on. Franklin had no previous criminal record. He hadn't bothered any of the townspeople, nor had he caused any kind of a disturbance. However, men couldn't be allowed to threaten the lives of duly appointed officers of the law, and a crime was quickly attached to Franklin.

A wide array of cutting and shooting instruments could be found upon the persons of many of the hardy citizens of frontier Arkansas—a state where legislators had once dueled with Bowie knives on the capitol grounds. According to a book put out by an Arkansas county board in 1888, "the law of the state prohibits the wearing or carrying of concealed weapons . . ."[2] Said law barred the concealed carry upon one's person of "any knife, dirk, sword-cane, brass knuckles, slung-shot or pistol (except the size used in the army and navy)."[3] The law appears to go as far back as statehood, as the Arkansas Supreme Court had upheld the ban on certain concealed weapons in 1842. Circuit court documents of the late 1880s list numerous defendants charged with "carrying weapons," which was the term for being found with a hideout gun or hidden blade.

Franklin's rifle was out in the open, but that didn't prevent the lawman from charging him with a violation of the weapons law. Perhaps the sheriff just ignored that fact, or perhaps Franklin had a knife or pocket pistol concealed in his clothing. One must remember that during those years in backwoods circuit courts, the actual state or federal laws could be a vague concept left to the notions of local lawmen or the judge and jury's decisions. Whatever the circumstances were, the sheriff wanted Franklin to face charges and placed him under arrest.

There wasn't a jail in Black Springs, so Sheriff Golden started toward the county seat at Mount Ida with his prisoner. Cogburn family lore has it that Franklin wasn't handcuffed on the nine-mile ride, either because the sheriff didn't have any restraints or because Sheriff Golden wasn't foolish enough to try to put that indignity on him.

The court records do not tell if Franklin was jailed when they arrived at Mount Ida or if he was chained to the iron band surrounding a giant shade tree on the courthouse lawn that sometimes served double duty as a tethering point for horses and a temporary place to constrain prisoners.[4] What is known is that during the January/February term of court, a circuit judge dug around in his mental junk box of the Arkansas legal code and found him guilty of "carrying a firearm," a misdemeanor offense. Franklin was fined fifty dollars, the minimum punishment for such a conviction.[5] Although the judge could have tapped him for the maximum $200 penalty, the indignity of his arrest and the infringement on his right to bear arms wasn't taken lightly. The Cogburns would later claim that the lawmen of the county were using Franklin as a whipping boy to try to assert their authority and that Judge Silas Vaught, a Confederate veteran, had a grudge against the former Union men of Montgomery County. While these claims may or may not have been true, the reason for Franklin's fine on such a trivial and questionable crime may have had more to do with the crackdown that had begun on the moonshiners of the county.

The minimum penalty or not, the fifty-dollar fine was truly

a hefty one, considering it was two times what most poor mountain folk made in a month if they were lucky enough to have a job or make a good crop. A criminal found guilty of making whiskey might only expect a $100 sentence from Judge Parker's federal court on a first offense. However, if Franklin was as unapologetic with the circuit judge as he was with the sheriff, perhaps he brought the verdict and fine on himself. Judges tend to frown on those who want to shoot the officers of the court.

What is certain is that nobody who knew Rooster believed that the trouble was over. Everyone in the mountains understood a blood feud, and no lawman was going to stop a killing when Deputy John D. Trammell and Rooster Cogburn met again. What they didn't know was how the troubles to come would be the talk of western Arkansas and pit the Hanging Judge and the Fort Smith court against an entire family.

2

The Cogburns

Hollywood, novels, and Depression-era comedians and radio personalities have embedded a laughable and sometimes despicable concept of the hillbilly into our collective American conscious. According to this line of thought, the mountains from West Virginia to Oklahoma are littered with "peculiar," backward people. However, many of the stereotypes—some even true—that were to make up the image of the hillbilly were not to come about until after the turn of the century. In truth, many of the original pioneers who came to Arkansas were nothing like the ignorant, incestuous offspring of Ma and Pa Kettle lounging barefoot around their whiskey stills that would one day come to represent what I like to call "mountain folk."

The Cogburns' story in America, like those of many other families, is a steady progression ever westward. The first of the family to arrive on the eastern shores of the Colonies were Lowland Scots who quickly accumulated holdings and social position as landowners and builders in the new nation being hacked out of the wilderness. Their name was Cockburn and their crest a fighting rooster.

The tax and land records of Virginia, North Carolina, and South Carolina give evidence of the Cockburns' early foothold in America. George Washington made note in his letters of his friend and neighbor Martin Cockburn.[6] While there is no evidence that Martin was of the line of Cockburns who came to Arkansas, his existence is indicative of their early arrival in America. John Franklin Cogburn's forefathers are found in the muster rolls of the Revolutionary War and the War of 1812.

By the early 1800s the Cockburns, some of whom had already began to change the spelling of their name to "Cogburn," were already spreading into Tennessee.[7] If the family had one strength it was an unusual preponderance of boy children, and those many sons needed breathing room and land of their own.

In the fall of 1859, two Cogburn brothers, Patrick and Henry, along with in-laws and friends, started west from Greene, Marion, and Sequatchie counties, Tennessee, in a wagon train.[8] There have always been tales of those fiddle-footed pioneers who couldn't stand it when their area began to get crowded and just had to move on to see what was over the next mountain. There is little evidence to explain why the Cogburn brothers left east Tennessee. Maybe they just needed more room than most folks or were looking for a fresh start, or the letters another brother sent them from Arkansas made the Bear State's bounty irresistible to them. Whatever their reasons, they started the long journey west to Arkansas.[9]

Patrick Cogburn and his best friend and brother-in-law, Washington Porter, led the wagon train over the muddy roads to Little Rock, Arkansas. Patrick brought his entire family with him, among them his two grown sons, Henry Page and John Wesley, Franklin Cogburn's father. Patrick's brother Henry also brought along his large family, including six sons (he would later sire more).

James Cogburn, Patrick and Henry's brother, had come from Georgia to settle along the Caddo River in west central

Arkansas a decade earlier.[10] It is possible that he was scouting out homestead sites for his extended family. From Little Rock, the Cogburn wagons creaked and groaned over the road to Mount Ida, crossing the Ouachita River and coming into the mountains proper. The route they took south from Mount Ida was more of a trail than a road, having been axed and shoveled through the forest years earlier.

Some months after their departure from Tennessee, the Cogburn wagon train arrived in a long, narrow valley along the Brushy Fork of the Caddo River. The hardwood and eastern pine timber of the Ouachita Mountains and the numerous clear streams and rivers looked like heaven to them, coming as they had from similar country in the mountains of east Tennessee. The soil on the mountainsides was thin and rocky, but the bottom lands along the little drainage valleys looked promising. Whitetail deer, turkeys, squirrels, ducks, and other wildlife were abundant, and the Cogburns and their in-laws and fellow immigrants stocked up on meat while they set in to build their homes before the worst of winter set in. Most of them located near the foot of a mountain overlooking the river, and the community of Fancy Hill came into being.

Less than an hour's ride to the east was a narrow gap in the mountains that the main channel of the Caddo River ran through. Hot springs bubbled up from the riverbed not far from "the Gap." Some historians have argued that the pass was the site of the Spanish explorer Hernando de Soto's battle with the Tula Indians in 1541.[11] The country was still wild enough that the last of the Caddo Indians in Arkansas lived along the river and wandered the mountains overlooking it. A store, post office, and water-driven gristmill had sprung up in the gap known as Centerville, or Gap Mills.[12] The post office was later moved a mile and half to the Bassinger Store, and Caddo Gap came into existence in 1878. Soon, it became known in mountain-speak simply as Caddy Gap.

Six or so miles to the north of Fancy Hill was Caddo Cove.[13] It was perhaps the oldest settlement in the area, boasting a whopping 165 citizens plus twenty-four slaves living there or in the six-square-mile area of the survey township, according to the 1830 U.S. census. Caddo Cove eventually faded away and Black Springs, a slightly younger settlement just down the road, took its place. The southern trail from Mount Ida to Dallas, Arkansas, passed through the scattering of buildings, and the traffic was heavy during the years just before and after the Civil War as land-hungry settlers migrated west.

Nine miles to the northeast of Black Springs was the town of Mount Ida. Originally, like all these settlements, it was nothing more than a combination store and post office, but in 1842 it became the county seat. By 1850 it boasted a two-story wooden-frame courthouse, more than one store, a hotel, and other places of business.

A long ride to the northwest into neighboring Polk County from the Cogburns' new home was Dallas, later renamed Mena with the coming of the railroad. The country due west of Fancy Hill and across the Little Missouri River was as wild as a peach orchard boar. For forty miles there were little more than a few scattered settlers, rough country, and owlhoot trails winding into the even bigger mountains at the eastern boundary of Indian Territory.

Montgomery County is fine country to this day, but there was a limited amount of bottom ground suitable for plowing. At the time the Cogburns arrived there were still parcels of arable land available, but for some reason most of the family chose homesteads in the shade of the mountains between the Caddo and Little Missouri rivers. It was as if something in that hidden, rugged country called to their nature.

While cotton may have been king in the South, the mountains of southwestern Arkansas were more suited to other types of agriculture. Early settlers farmed small plots of corn and grew gardens for their sustenance. Hogs turned loose to feed on acorns could be recaptured and fed out for curing in log smokehouses carved into the hillside. Other than vegetables and pork, and maybe a milk cow, the Cogburns' larder came from the land. Blackberries, huckleberries, and muscadines could be gathered during the summer, and acorns and hickory nuts in the fall. They learned where the banana-like papaws grew on the shady north slopes of the mountains and that the sassafras, polk salad, chicory, and wild asparagus they had known in their former home grew in Arkansas also.

The rivers teemed with fish, and a man with a keen eye and a straight-shooting rifle didn't have to hunt far for game in the woodlands. A call made from a wing bone or a cedar box could imitate the putt, cluck, and purr of a hen turkey and fool a springtime gobbler into shooting range. Deer meat was fine eating, but a lean diet of venison often left mountain people craving fat. Hogs weren't the only source of lard, as the mountains were thick with black bear. Not only could a hunter get plenty of fat meat if he killed one, but he also gained a fine rug or robe for his bed.

Although settlers began trickling into what would become Montgomery County by the early 1830s, the country was still plenty wild and short of some of the civilizing influences older population centers bragged about. Without the tax base resulting from a large population of deeded landowners, there was little the state of Arkansas could provide in the way of services. The road system was often impassable in foul weather, law enforcement sometimes nonexistent, and citizens quickly learned that they had to rely on their own wits and hard work.

The Cogburns had no gripes about being left alone to live their lives as they saw fit. They had been pioneering for generations and were nothing if not independent. Government didn't build your home, make your clothes, hunt your meat, put in your crops, or defend your life. The only thing the government was good for was to tax what little hard-earned money they could procure. When it came to the Law, a man rolled his own from the makings of his individual ideas of right and wrong. The only authority the Cogburn clan recognized was God and a gun.

The next generation of Cogburn men grew up in the mountains toting guns and making their own way in wild country without asking anything from anyone. They weren't rich by any banker's ledger, but they were proud men who matched the hard, rocky ground they called home. Schools were spotty or nonexistent, but the land itself provided an education for each and every one of them. They learned the mountains like the back of their hands, and nature taught them that a man had to fight to stay alive. Some kind of trouble was always at hand, and a man of any account was ready to handle it.

Such thinking was great for pioneers, but the same rugged individualists who could thrive on the frontier often chafed under the structure of civilization when it finally came. Long before law and order and the state reached deep into the mountains during the years after the hard times of the Civil War, many of its oldest citizens were set in their ways. The early mountain folk of the county had been living just fine without courts or lawyers telling them what they could or couldn't do.

Short of revenue during the Civil War, the United States Congress in 1862 imposed excise taxes on alcohol and required distillers to have a federal license. After the war, newly appointed district tax collectors in the Southern states employed revenue agents to arrest those who made untaxed moonshine. These federal agents were the "revenuers" of mountain folklore. In addition to the revenuers, the Western District of Arkansas sent out deputy marshals to enforce the federal whiskey laws. Many of the revenuers assigned to western Arkansas were also sworn in as Deputy U.S. Marshals.

Taxing the whiskey a man made seemed more like the action

of a tyrant than a democratic government or a free republic to some hill folks. Making a living in the mountains was hard enough, and having to gain approval and purchase a license from the state or federal government to distill and sell liquor made no more sense than having to buy a license to cook their own food. Folks made moonshine because they needed money, and then the government would come along and fine them for making it. The fines were money the moonshiners obviously didn't have, or they might not have been making 'shine in the first place. If you were caught with your still, you could always build another to help pay the courts.

American frontiersmen could be testy, independent sorts who were slow to give up any of what they considered their God-given freedoms, as President George Washington found out in the Whiskey Rebellion of the 1790s. It took the assemblage of troops and the threat of force to bring western Pennsylvania distillers into line during those years, and there would come a time in Arkansas when a certain judge in Fort Smith would sometimes think he too needed an army to quell his own whiskey rebellion.

Nobody knows when the Cogburns started making whiskey. They may well have made it back in Tennessee, or learned after their arrival in Arkansas. Perhaps it was a tradition and skill their forbearers had brought with them from Scotland. No matter where or when the Cogburns learned it, the fact remains that some of the clan made whiskey and nobody, government or not, was going to tell them they couldn't. This was especially true for the Cogburn they called Rooster and a few of his kinfolk.

3

Parker's Boys

On March 18, 1875, a thirty-six-year-old portly Ohioan and former Missouri congressman arrived in Fort Smith, Arkansas. Isaac Charles Parker had been appointed by President Ulysses S. Grant as the new federal judge for the Western District of Arkansas, and he didn't take long to make his mark. He started to work ten days after his arrival, and by the end of the May term of court he had sentenced eight murderers to death. On September 3, 1875, he hung six of them simultaneously. Just for good measure, on April 21, 1876, five more killers stood side by side on his gallows to be strung up before a crowd estimated at over seven thousand people—it would have been another sextet except for a presidential reprieve granted at the last minute to one of the sentenced.[14]

Until 1883, when his jurisdiction was divided between Fort Smith and two other courts in Texas and Kansas, there was no appeal from his rulings except to the President of the United States. Seventy-nine men were hung during his time on the bench.[15] While there was much more to Judge Parker than the myth of the Bible-thumping zealot created by newspapers and folklore, it can't be denied that he was indeed the "Hanging Judge."

It can be argued, however, that Isaac Parker was the proper man for the job. The area he presided over would have chewed up softer men, less devoted to duty and justice. In 1871, Congress had created a separate federal judgeship for the Western District of Arkansas—an area consisting of over 74,000 square miles of Indian Territory (later Oklahoma) and eighteen of the western counties of Arkansas.[16] The headquarters for the court were located in Fort Smith, a burgeoning city and shipping port along the Arkansas River. The former judge of the district, William Story, had led an ineffective carpetbagger court, known more for graft and corruption than for meting out justice. While that court was languishing and wallowing in political squabbles and congressional investigations, its jurisdiction was virtually overflowing with outlaws and delinquents the likes of which America had never seen assembled all in one place. Pistol poppers, pimps, prostitutes, poisoners, whiskey peddlers, holdup men, rapists, con men, gamblers, train wreckers, rustlers, knife artists, renegade savages, cutthroats, chicken thieves, and just about every kind of miscreant in between called the Western District of Arkansas home. Perhaps author Glenn Shirley said it best when he wrote, "There was no worse spawning place for Satan's own on the western frontier."[17]

The rugged Sans Bois, Winding Stair, and Kiamichi mountains lay just to the west and southwest of Fort Smith, the Boston Mountains, Cookson Hills, and the southern tip of the Ozarks to the north and northwest, and the Ouachita Mountains to the south. The rugged vastness of these rocky, timbered mountains provided perfect haunts and hideouts for outlaws. The country farther west into Indian Territory was just as littered with gun-toting felons and would-be criminals. River bottom thickets, cedar breaks, and miles of red clay prairies scattered between the dense, low brush of the Cross Timbers gave almost as much cover to fugitives and highwaymen as the mountains.

The boundaries of Indian Territory had been formed for the Five Civilized Tribes—Choctaw, Chickasaw, Cherokee, Creek, and Seminole—when they were forcibly removed from the Southeastern United States. In 1870, the Osage had grown tired of being continuously shoved off their latest land by the government and purchased a reservation in Indian Territory from their longtime enemy, the Cherokees.[18] Later, reservations for the Apache and many of the plains tribes such as the Comanche, Kiowa, Arapaho, and Cheyenne were formed in the western half of the block. More tribes were relocated alongside each other, and by 1890 there were at least thirty-two tribes residing within Judge Parker's jurisdiction.

Despite Indian Territory supposedly belonging to the tribes who had been relocated there, the Texas Road and the Butterfield stagecoach route south from Missouri saw heavy traffic even before the Civil War. The California Trail from Fort Smith to Santa Fe had been a thoroughfare since the 49er gold rush. The Katy (M. K. & T./Missouri-Kansas-Texas) railroad had been built across Indian Territory starting in 1871, and the Choctaw Indians had granted coal concessions around McAlester in the years to follow. Soon after, outsiders were pouring across the border like water—the good and the bad.

It was a veritable mixing pot of nationalities and ethnicities—white, red, and black. The freed slaves of many of the Five Civilized Tribes were granted tribal membership or stayed in the area at the end of the Civil War, and perhaps nowhere in America was the pioneering effort of African Americans more apparent than in the wilds of the Indian Territory. Italian miners, Irish tracklayers, and English and Texas cattle barons bellied up to the bar for glasses of Choc beer, and their accents were no stranger than the guttural languages of natives standing beside them. Many non-Indians had married into the Five Civilized Tribes, thus gaining the right to operate legally within tribal lands. While many of the marriages were for love, others were attempts by crooked men to gain a foothold to steal timber or engage in other nefarious dealings. By the mid-1880s, the Cherokees and some of the plains tribes in the western half of the Indian Territory were leasing their lands and reservations to Texas and Kansas cattleman. Wild cowboys manned line camps and dugouts scattered from the Canadian to the Red.

The tribal courts were to take care of their own members, but all crimes involving U.S. citizens or disagreements between the tribes fell under the jurisdiction of the Hanging Judge. The Indian Intercourse Act of 1834 had laid many of the ground rules for the legal treatment of Indian Territory, but applying that law to what was known as the Indian Nations, or simply "the Nations," was easier said than done. Murder and robbery were rampant, and not usually the romanticized sort portrayed in Western movies and dime novels. It is not far from fact to say that just as many victims died from axes and clubs at the hands of petty thieves and drunks as did from the blazing guns of train robbers and holdup men. For every instance of gunfights and midnight rides over express payrolls and bank loot, there are recorded court cases of men and women being murdered for watermelons, their clothing, or a jug of whiskey.[19] A dramatic blood-and-gore headline in the September 9, 1885, *Arkansas Gazette* read, FIFTEEN MURDERS IN INDIAN TERRITORY LAST MONTH.

For many years, Western novelists avoided writing about the Indian Territory with any factual basis, despite it having all the necessary ingredients for the genre—settlers, Indian wars, outlaws, railroads, cattle drives, etc. Storytelling icon and author Louis L'Amour often expressed his distaste for many of the outlaws and the crimes of the old Indian Territory. Despite its qualifications, the bloody ground of the Nations often didn't match the romantic ideas of what the American Frontier was all about. All the glorious pioneering spirit was there in spades, but in the mythical Old West of the silver screen, rapes were rare, villains often had honor, and only the rarest of low-down dogs and assassins shot men in the back. Any researcher poring over the historical documents of Indian Territory quickly finds that Judge Parker's jurisdiction broke all those rules. While it must be said that there were good, honest settlers calling the Indian Territory home, it is also safe to say that for better than seventy years the country was undoubtedly the wildest, most bloodthirsty chunk of real estate west of the Mississippi.

One of the only things keeping the outlaws' numbers down was their propensity for killing each other off. While gentlemen had once dueled to defend their honor, the badmen of the Indian Nations couldn't or wouldn't wait for such formalities when they were in a killing mood. If someone crossed them they just naturally took hold of what was handy to quickly and mortally end the disagreement. One such altercation pitted Charles Johnson against Sam Starr, two frontier toughs. Portions of the witnesses' sworn affidavits to the court examiner are as follows:

> On the 15th day of December, 1871, the defendant [Charles Johnson] & Sam Starr got to quarreling in the Cherokee Nation, Western District of Arkansas. They passed the lie and the damned son of a bitch [Johnson], our defendant, struck Sam Starr with a chopping axe.
>
> —Harry Starr

> Sam Starr made a grab at the axe with one hand and put his hand on his knife with the other and

> the defendant cut him with the axe on the left
> side. . . . I saw his guts through the hole.
>
> —Callis West

Charles Johnson, hoping to avoid being charged with assault with intent to kill, had a different take on the fight:

> [Johnson] was peacefully at work clearing his
> new land when the difficulty arose. Starr
> advanced on him with a drawn knife and he re-
> treated. In attempting to ward off Starr the cut
> was inflicted.
>
> —Charles Johnson

As if to point out that Sam Starr was no timid innocent himself, it is also noted matter-of-factly that:

> Sam always carries a butcher knife.
>
> —Mose Johnson and Dr. J. C. Fields
> December 16, 1872, I.T.[20]

Sam Starr had his wounds stitched up by Dr. Fields and survived to fight another day, although he may have avoided men with sharp, double-bit axes in the future.[21] Charles Johnson jumped his $400 bail and was never brought to trial for chopping men up like firewood. He was just one of many cut-and-shoot desperadoes way out yonder in the Indian Nations.

By the time Judge Parker came to the bench, the outlawry was giving new meaning to the term "the Wild West." Not only did the terrain help hide lawbreakers, but the outlaws' sheer numbers provided a sort of asylum. It was next to impossible for a lawman to travel in search of criminals without the country grapevine spreading word of his coming. Many of those living in the Nations and western Arkansas who weren't outlaws themselves gave aid and information to criminal sorts, either out of fear or for profit. Many of the Native Americans there had little or nothing to say to any white man. Talk had never gotten them anything but lies when dealing with their pale conquerors.

American soldiers during the Vietnam War often referred to jungles full of Viet Cong as "Indian Country"—a metaphor for hostile terrain born out of the Old West. Official indictment forms from Parker's court listed the name of the indicted, the charge, and the location, designated as "in the Indian Country."[22] Newspapers and letters of the time referred to the area the same way. A portion of the district court's jurisdiction did belong to Native Americans, but considering all things, it is easy to find double meaning in the term. Truly, Judge Parker's bailiwick was a place where you could lose your scalp. It was six-shooter country; it was the land of the James-Younger Gang, the Doolins and Daltons, the Starrs, and a thousand other renegades lesser known but equally vicious.

There was Crawford Goldsby, alias Cherokee Bill, as wild and gun-happy as an outlaw came. He was part white, part black, part French, part Cherokee, and all bad. After he was locked away in the U.S. jail at Fort Smith he was given an empty Winchester to pose with for a picture. Afterward, he worked the lever and pulled the trigger on the harmless weapon so fast as to amaze the observing lawmen around him. He told his admirers that he wasn't always accurate with his blazing speed, but he could lay down enough fire to keep his enemies too nervous to shoot back at him properly. When Cherokee Bill made his famous escape attempt from the jail, it is said he gobbled like a turkey, the traditional Cherokee battle cry, while he shot at the guards.

John Billee was so mean and fierce he had to be chained in a corner of the jail.[23] While held prisoner by lawmen on the way to Fort Smith after his capture, he managed to slip his cuffs and kill one deputy marshal and severely wound another. On the other hand, murderer Daniel Evans was pleasant and likeable after being caught by deputies. But the same smiling man had killed his friend for his boots and horse and bragged to fellow inmates that he had once held burning pine pitch to an old man's feet in order to make him tell where his stash of money was hidden.[24]

Tangdhangtanka, or the Panther, was an Osage madman and serial killer. His face was scarred until it was beyond human, his teeth filed to points, and his hair was long and tangled like some beast's. He wore the remains of shackles around his wrists from a former imprisonment by his tribe. He murdered men, women, and children and took their trinkets and skulls for trophies back to his cave.[25]

Horse thievery was an everyday occurrence in Parker's district. A steady stream of stolen horses worked back and forth from north to south and east to west. A horse swiped in Kansas could be sold with no questions asked in Texas, and vice versa. The Nations were littered with outlaw relay stations, strongholds, and holding pens where "hot" ponies could be held to cool a while. An honest, smart citizen traveled the country roads warily, made his fire hidden in the brush, and slept with a hold on his mount and one eye open if he valued his life and property.

From the Civil War until well after the turn of the century, a man packing a badge found little love once he rode out of Fort Smith to enforce the law. Regardless, Judge Parker intended to scowl and whack his gavel until every villain in his jurisdiction was either in prison or twisting in the air by his neck. It says something about the time and place that after twenty-one years at his post, he still hadn't run out of outlaws to hang.

But the Hanging Judge could have never plied his trade were it not for the hard-riding devils who pinned a badge on their vests and set out into the wilds to bring back the indicted and the accused. The Deputy U.S. Marshals who rode out of Fort Smith were far more than men with big mustaches and tall hats, bristling with firearms. They came from varying backgrounds and had their own individual skills and modes of operation. While many of them did become gunmen of some skill, others dealt out law and order more with cunning detective work and cautious ambush. But one thing they all had in common was nerve, and lots of it.

Heck Thomas, Bill Tilghman, Bass Reeves, Frank Canton— some of these peace officers became as famous as the desperadoes they chased from hell to breakfast. For nothing more than fees and mileage and an occasional reward if they were lucky, they set out alone or in small posses to serve subpoenas and scour the brush for badmen. They risked life and limb with every step their ponies took along uncertain and dangerous trails. Many were their enemies and few were their friends where they had to ride.

Often, the only allies the deputy marshals had were the Indian lawmen. Each of the Five Civilized Tribes employed Lighthorsemen to patrol their individual nations. By the late 1880s, the federal government kept a force in the field headquartered out of Muskogee known as the U.S. Indian Police. Some tribes, such as the Choctaws, had sheriffs for each of the districts within their nation. The plains tribes to the west also kept their own policemen patrolling their reservations.

Although the tribal courts had no authority over non-tribe members, they could make arrests of white people and hand them over to the U.S. court. Often they joined forces with the Deputy U.S. Marshals to form posses big enough to combat some of the stronger outlaw gangs. Their knowledge of the people and the terrain of the Indian Country was a boon to Parker's boys in locating fugitives. In later years, some of the tribal lawmen were sworn in as Deputy U.S. Marshals or express agents, carrying multiple badges.

No one wanted the foreign criminals captured or extradited more than the Indians themselves. A tribal court could hand down whippings or executions to its own citizens, but wasn't allowed to try or punish white Americans depredating within their boundaries. Their supposedly sovereign nations were overrun with the bad folks they were legally helpless to stop by civilized means. Occasionally, the tribal lawmen didn't wait to hand over prisoners to the federal representatives at Fort Smith. If the outlaws were foolish enough to fight back, nobody was going to question the death of thugs killed in a gun battle, even if they died at the hands of Indians. The federal court didn't take much notice if some especially bothersome outlaws were occasionally found hanging by their necks from trees.

An old descendant of a Choctaw Lighthorseman used to tell stories of ghosts and outlaws to the children around Talihina, Oklahoma. One of his favorite tales was of a horse thief his grandfather had helped hang in the 1870s. The bandit kept swearing that he was a white man while the noose was being tightened around his neck and his horse positioned under a high tree limb. The Lighthorse posse paid heed to his claims of immunity and rode off. Accidentally, of course, they forgot to take the rope off his neck, and his horse walked out from under him to follow them. The outlaw was left dangling in what might be called a precarious position. According to the old-timer who told the story, "Even if the horse thief was a white man, he looked Indian enough that nobody passing by would have questioned his nationality enough to raise a stink about his hanging."

Some of the Lighthorsemen and the U.S. Indian Police became as famous in their day as the Hanging Judge's deputy marshals. Some of those men were Choctaws, such as the Limestone Gap lawman Charles Leflore. He probably single-handedly caught more desperadoes than any man in the Nations. The Cherokees had Sam Sixkiller, Frank West, and the gunfighter Jackson Ellis.[26] The Creeks had the famous Yuchi tracker Tiger Jack. Little has been written of these men and their fight against lawlessness, but a careful historian will notice that Indian lawmen were present during many of the well-known manhunts and arrests in the Indian Territory.

Those outlaws that Parker's deputy marshals sought to arrest weren't impressed or awed with badges, and the worst of them saw the tin shield on a lawman's vest as nothing more than a rifle target. A Fort Smith newspaper article of the day, repeating an Indian Territory article, gives a clue to the kind of badmen these deputies were up against:

> The Chieftain gives the full swing particulars of the recent killing of Joe Sky at Prairie City, Cherokee Nation. Grindstone, a Shawnee, had a revolver and laying it down remarked, "I have one of them things now." Sky replied that he "ate them kind of things," to which the other ventured the assertion that he could give him a dose he could not eat. Sky answered, "I'll bet you $10 you can't," whereupon Grindstone shot him dead and rode off.[27]

Truly, life was cheap out beyond the city limits of the frontier metropolis of Fort Smith. There were some salty sorts out in the hinterlands who wouldn't throw down their guns and say "uncle" just because a lawman showed up with a writ for their arrest. Time and time again, the newspapers of the day report deputy marshals hailing some house during one of their manhunts and being immediately greeted by gunfire. During the days of Parker's court, when the bad folks scoffed at law and order and bold men with badges rode to give them battle, at least sixty-nine deputy marshals were killed in the line of duty.[28]

Records of the U.S. Marshal's office of the era are sketchy and incomplete, and often it is only through court records and newspaper articles that it can be determined actually who wore badges for the Hanging Judge. For every deputy marshal whose name would one day be made famous, there were countless others putting their lives on the line to bring law and order to the Western District of Arkansas. In addition to the sworn-in deputy marshals, many of Parker's manhunters had associates whom they employed regularly as posse members. The names of these men weren't entered into the official books, only their fees, for which the deputy marshals invoiced the government.

And of all the crimes that took up both the court's and the deputies' time and attention, liquor law violations were right up next to the top. In the mountains and dark canyons of Cogburn country, the moonshining had gotten plumb out of hand. The Cogburns apparently considered themselves the only law south of the Ouachita River. Franklin "Rooster" Cogburn's willingness to kill a Deputy U.S. Marshal had proven that. The Hanging Judge needed a man to ride down there and set things straight. He needed a man who already knew the country and the clan of outlaw mountain men defying him. If law and order was going to hold sway in the Western District of Arkansas, the Cogburns were going to have to be brought to justice.

John David Trammell, or J. D., was one of the men who

pinned on a badge and took the oath of office in Fort Smith. He already knew Montgomery County well from his previous detective work there and had little love for the Cogburns. He was more than willing to go back and smoke them out and drag them off to Fort Smith at the Hanging Judge's pleasure.

Deputy U.S. Marshal Trammell was born November 10, 1837, in Crawford County, Arkansas, and was a Confederate veteran. Like many folks, his family had lived through trials and tribulations. He was the only living son of Peter Trammell and Mary Smoot, a blind woman.[29] After the Civil War, Trammell apparently spent time farther south, as he married his first wife, Clara Andrews, in December 1865, in Hopkins, Texas. According to Trammell family folklore, Clara herself had seen hard times, as her father had been killed by Confederate guerrillas, or bushwhackers, in Arkansas sometime during the early years of the war. Clara passed away in 1877, and Trammell married Mary Neal, only to lose her in 1884.[30] Several children were born to each marriage. By the late 1880s when he served Parker's court, his blind mother was taking care of the children still at home.

Trammell, according to some of his descendants and the evidence of his actions, was a determined and sometimes reckless man when it came to doing his duty. For months in 1887 he had worked undercover among the Cogburns and other families in Montgomery County in an attempt to determine who was and who wasn't making moonshine. He was wise enough to recognize that many were beginning to suspect him of being a lawman, and he left the area to present his evidence to his superiors in Fort Smith. His sworn testimony against the Cogburns was just what the Hanging Judge wanted, and a posse was organized to raid into Cogburn Country.

It is unknown when Trammell took the oath as a deputy marshal, but his signature is found on writs of arrest for the U.S. Marshal's office as early as 1886. Coincidentally, these writs of arrest were served on moonshiners in the southern part of Yell County, some of whom were allied with the Cogburn's operation or distant kin by marriage. It is possible that the feud between Trammell and the Cogburns went farther back than his undercover detective work in 1887.

On June 25, 1888, Trammell and fifteen other lawmen from the U.S. Marshal's office, revenuers, and posse members rode into the mountains of far southwest Montgomery County.[31] Apparently, the posse was expecting a large haul of criminals, for they took along a wagon. A *Fort Smith Elevator* newspaper article for July 6, 1888, mentions the posse's wagon. The lawmen probably employed a driver who could serve double duty as a camp guard and cook for any prisoners taken. Almost every posse of this type did just that, unless they were hot and heavy on the trail of fast-traveling bandits. Deputy marshals could make much more money per trip if they joined together and attempted to haul in a wagonload of criminals. The deputy marshals could employ additional posse members, and the lawmen often had favorites who worked with them regularly. Mileage and expenses for manpower, feeding prisoners, etc. could be charged to the government.

On that morning, near Black Springs, the posse came upon some moonshiners at work. The men they surrounded at the still threw up their hands and surrendered without resistance. During the course of the morning the posse destroyed three stills and placed five men under arrest. Franklin Cogburn's older brother, Bill, was one of the prisoners.[32] And perhaps none of the deputy marshals realized that they had just begun a fight that would take years to settle.

4

Man of the Times

Psychologists, sociologists, and a host of studious historians have long pointed out that much of the violence of the Old West was due to the experiences of men coming home from the Civil War, whiskey, a lack of justice and its institutions along the frontier, and Old Testament notions of "an eye for an eye, and a tooth for a tooth." All those things being considered, Franklin Cogburn was, indeed, a man of the times—shaped and molded in a bloody, hardscrabble mold just like a piece of mountain clay.

Franklin's father, John Wesley Cogburn, had not been long in Montgomery County when the Civil War broke out in 1861. He was twenty-one years old, hard at work building a farm and family, and wanted no part of a war that didn't seem to concern him. While there were many men of the county who joined right up with old Jeff Davis's boys in gray, John Wesley wasn't one of them. He would just as soon settle down next door to his parents and siblings with the pretty little Georgia girl he'd married in December. She gave him a fine baby boy the following year.

He and his family never saw much of the government and certainly never got any help from it. And then the state of Arkansas seceded and had the audacity to want him to fight for the Confederacy. Neither he nor his family owned slaves, and none of them had much understanding of the squabble about states' rights. Like mountain folk in parts of Tennessee and Kentucky, the war seemed far away and a rich man's fight at best. The thought of a bunch of Yankee boys riding down from the north and taking over Arkansas stirred up most folks, but not enough for all of the Montgomery County men to throw down their plows and axes and march off to war. It was hard work from sunup to sundown to keep a family from starving, and going off and getting shot on some far-off battlefield didn't make much sense. There were some fire-eaters who immediately joined up with one side or the other, mostly Confederate, but in the early years of the war many citizens of the county limited their participation to standing around post offices and debating the subject.

By 1863 the Union controlled everything north and east of the Arkansas River, while the Confederacy held the territory to the south and west.[33] The Union was doing everything in its power to press into the southwestern portions of the state. A few larger-scale battles were fought during the Camden campaign, but for the most part, the fighting in and around Montgomery County was small skirmishes. Confederate and Union troops alike traveled the roads, often donning their enemy's uniforms when necessary for disguise. Much has been made of Missouri and its split during the war, but Arkansas was almost as bad. Guerrilla fighters raped, looted, and murdered at whim throughout the countryside. Gangs of Union sympathizing cutthroats were known as jayhawkers, and their Confederate counterparts were known as bushwhackers. Neither kind of raider could be readily recognized when they rode up to some poor soul's farm. The terrified civilian who shaded his eyes from his corn or cotton patch and watched strangers approach his home often couldn't tell friend from foe. The riders he saw approaching might be Union soldiers in Confederate uniforms or vice versa, jayhawkers or bushwhackers. A wily man made his best guess and hoped he claimed the correct side of the fight, Union or Southern. As the ferryman in *The Outlaw Josey Wales* says, a man had to be able to "sing the 'Battle Hymn of the Republic' or 'Dixie' with equal enthusiasm, depending upon present company."[34] But that wouldn't necessarily save a person, even if he was exceptionally musically talented and picked the correct tune for the moment. Many of the guerrilla fighters didn't care which army you sympathized with and simply used the war as an excuse to murder and pillage.

The mountains of southwestern Arkansas had never had much law and order, but during the years of the war there was virtually none at all. If a citizen could avoid the soldiers and killers prowling the roads, the Confederate Home Guard was to be feared almost as much. As the war progressed and the South became hard-pressed for fighting men, many a man in Arkansas was conscripted into the Confederate forces by either regular troops or the Home Guard running dragnets to gather able-bodied reinforcements, willing or not. Conscription meant you got a gun, maybe a uniform, damned little to eat at times, and lots of promised pay that might never arrive. If you were paid, the Confederate scrip was virtually worthless by the last years of the war.

Arkansas may have joined the Confederacy, but Montgomery County harbored more than a few Union sympathizers. These men became known as Mountain Federals. The Cogburns and many of their neighbors and in-laws were such men. Early in 1864, John Wesley Cogburn and his brother Page decided that there was no dodging the fight and traveled north to Waldron, Arkansas. Explanations for the Cogburns' choice of sides in the war have long since been lost to the family. However, the fact is that John Wesley and Page, and a few other Montgomery County boys, went up into Sebastian County and joined up with the Union.[35]

Henry Page Cogburn may have been the younger of the brothers by two years, but at twenty-two, he didn't have to stand behind anybody when it came to a scrap. Upon arriving in Arkansas, he built his cabin so far back in the mountains that the "birds don't sing," as is the mountain saying. His only neighbors were bears, but he spent more time skinning them than talking to them. In a clan full of hairy-chested, bull-stubborn, tough men he was the fellow everybody walked wide around if he was feeling ornery. Not so many years ago, old-timers down Caddy Gap and Greasy Cole way would tell you that. Some of those rheumy-eyed, weathered men would scratch behind the bibs of their overalls and recall that Page had perhaps been a jayhawker, or a guerrilla fighter for one side or the other at the very least.[36] If there ever was any evidence of that, it has long since been lost or buried with those who lived alongside him in those olden years. His being labeled as a jayhawker may have had more to do with the multiple uses of the term during the war years. If you were of Southern sympathies, a jayhawker in Montgomery County could be either a raider or simply a Mountain Federal.[37]

And there are still folks living in Montgomery County, Cogburns and others, who swear that it was Page who led the raid that burned Albert Pike's home and ran him out of the country in an attempt to steal the Confederate gold he had embezzled. Pike was an early-day Western explorer, veteran of the Mexican-American War, noted lawyer, and Masonic leader. When Arkansas seceded from the Union, he was appointed a brigadier general in the Confederacy. He was assigned to raise and lead native troops in the Indian Territory and was in constant conflict with higher-ranking officers. In 1862, his superiors charged that he mismanaged his forces at the Battle of Pea

Ridge (Elkhorn Tavern). His Cherokee troops were said to have stopped to scalp fallen Union troops, slowing the Confederate advance when the fight was going its way and turning a sure victory into defeat. Coupled with this accusation were charges that he was embezzling large amounts of Confederate funds. This squabble of generals led to Pike's resignation in July of 1862. He owned a fine home in Little Rock but decided to seek a retreat in the mountains of Montgomery County. In the fall of that year he purchased a farm at Greasy Cole along the Little Missouri River, not far from Page's homestead.

Supposedly, Pike flashed around too much coin in the area, and Page Cogburn plotted how to get some of it. Pike was warned that marauders were coming to rob him, and he and his slaves hurriedly loaded what they could fit in a buggy and fled in the night, driving wildly through the mountains and nearly drowning at a crossing on the Caddo River.[38] Pike survived to publish the Masonic tome *Morals and Dogma of the Ancient and Accepted Scottish Rite of Freemasonry,* which he wrote while in the mountains. He practiced law from New York to Memphis in the years that followed and is also often given the dubious honor of helping found the Ku Klux Klan. Despite his troubles in the Ouachita Mountains, he lived to the ripe old age of eighty-two, dying in 1891 in Washington D.C., where his fellow Masons erected a statue of him. The Cogburns and other Montgomery County settlers of the era couldn't testify to any of the events of Pike's later life, for the last time they saw the general he was still whipping his horses out of the mountains with his eyes wide and his white beard flapping over his shoulders in the wind.[39]

Many modern-day treasure hunters believe that Pike was a high-ranking member of the secret Confederate society and branch of the Masons, the Knights of the Golden Circle. The KGC supposedly plotted and instigated the Civil War as a means to power and the permanent institution of slavery. Furthermore,

Pike and former bushwhackers and outlaws such as Jesse James are said to have cached gold both during and after the war to fund a revival of the rebellion in the future. Investigative journalist Warren Getler and KGC enthusiast and devout treasure hunter Bob Brewer claim in their book, *Rebel Gold,* that it was Page Cogburn who attacked General Pike's home and that Confederate gold is buried in the Ouachita Mountains.[40]

In truth, raiders took Pike's son hostage elsewhere in Arkansas and later in 1863 burned the general's mountain retreat in an attempt to get his alleged hoard of treasure. However, beyond the KGC conspiracy sleuths' assertions and the folklore of the mountains, there is no documentation to prove that Page was the leader of the bad guys. It seems strange and unbelievable that Page would steal a treasure worth a fortune and then leave it behind to march off to war less than a year later.

There are also unproven tales that Cole Younger came to hide out around Caddy Gap during a break he and the James boys took from robbing banks, trains, and coaches. Supposedly Cole posed as a doctor in the community until it was safe to join back up with Jesse and Frank. And wouldn't you know it? There were those who claimed that Page and Cole became good friends, possibly having known each other from their days back in the Civil War. No matter the truth behind any of those old wives' tales, the legend remains, and it is safe to say that Page Cogburn was a man with "the bark on."

Little has been passed down through the family about the kind of man John Wesley was, beyond the story of his time in the war. If there ever were any photos of him, they have long since been lost to his descendants. His only legacy are his service records from the Civil War and the faces of his sons. If he was anything like his brother, it might be safe to say that the two of them went north without any doubt that they could handle whatever fate brought their way. As it was, the war was to shape their destiny—and their families'—for years to come.

But in the spring of 1864, things didn't look so bad for the two. The supply sergeant outfitted them with good Sharps carbines and uniforms and paid them in Yankee gold.[41] Their regiment, the 2nd Kansas Cavalry, was mostly stationed far away from the fierce fighting in the East.[42] Duty for L Company in western Kansas and the northeastern corner of Indian Territory meant boring patrols of the Osage Trace and Texas Road from Fort Scott to Fort Gibson and on to Fort Smith. They were there to protect supply lines from the Confederate Indian forces under the Cherokee Brigadier General Stand Watie. Mostly it was post duty, as the Union controlled their forts and the Confederates roamed the countryside at will.[43] While there was some chance of encountering those crafty hit-and-run fighters, the Union soldiers were relatively safe behind their walls or in large forces patrolling north of Fort Gibson. The risk of getting shot by a Johnny Reb out west wasn't near as bad as it would have been on some cannonball-pitted battlefield over in Louisiana or Mississippi. John Wesley and Page were assigned a good horse apiece and were getting to see some pretty new country. They were getting paid regularly and eating three squares a day, and army living didn't seem too bad if all they had to worry about was a handful of untrained, ragged Indians pestering Union supply lines. Neither one of those mountain boys knew a thing about General Stand Watie.

The Civil War had devastated the Five Civilized Tribes. As soon as the Southern states seceded from the Union, emissaries uniformed in both blue and gray were sent among them to gain their aid in the war to come. With the exception of the Choctaws, there was bitter intertribal division between Union and Confederate loyalties. The early battles in that country were Indian versus Indian, and members of the same tribe became enemies.[44]

Despite their forced removal to the Western lands in the early 1800s, the Five Civilized Tribes had miraculously rebuilt much of what they lost back East, both homes and livelihoods. Before the Civil War, many of the more well-to-do tribesmen owned fine homes and frontier plantations in Indian Territory, some with African American slaves doing the labor. They ran large herds of cattle on open range. The countryside was dotted with the cabins of those of more modest income, and those structures were surrounded by cotton and other crops. By late 1862 the Indian Territory was a no-man's-land with nothing left but devastation, refugees, and warring factions. Families went to Kansas or Texas for safety, depending on where their loyalties lay. Crops were left abandoned, livestock strayed or was stolen, homes burned, and people starved or froze in the bitter cold of winter as they fled from the wrath of war.

Stand Watie was a weathered veteran long before the war began. He had fought in the Cherokees' own civil war many years earlier.[45] He was an expert in the ways of the small-unit guerrilla tactics favored by his people. He organized and commanded the Cherokee Mounted Rifles for the Confederacy from the start of the war and continued to fight for the South even after some of his tribe swapped allegiances and swore loyalty to the Union in 1862.

Stand Watie was the rare officer who was always at the front of his men in battle. Under his leadership, the Indian troops were a force to be reckoned with. During the first year of the war his regiment almost single-handedly ran the pro-Union Indian forces out of the Territory in one wild skirmish after another. After proving himself as a commander at the more conventional and large-scale battles of Wilson's Creek and Pea Ridge, he was soon leading a combined force of Cherokee, Choctaw, Chickasaw, Seminole, Creek, and Osage troops. On May 6, 1864, he was made a brigadier general in command of the 1st Indian Brigade, Army of the Trans-Mississippi. He is the only Native American to achieve that rank in the military history of the United States.

His bold, hard-riding troops matched his lightning-quick hit-and-run tactics. After the Confederate forces' defeat at the Battle of Honey Springs and their loss of Fort Smith and Fort Gibson, he was the sole menace to the Union in the Indian Territory. He played havoc with their supply lines, feinting attack at one place and striking at another. In 1864 he was at the height of his prowess and power. On June 15, he captured the federal steamboat *J. R. Williams* in a cannon ambush five miles below the confluence of the South Canadian and Arkansas rivers. The loot his men carried away cost the Union in excess of $120,000, and much-needed supplies. No man was wanted dead by the Union more than General Stand Watie, and although the South was defeated, the Union never brought him to bay. He was the last general to surrender at the close of the war, doing so on June 23, 1865, nearly three months after Appomattox.

The Union controlled Indian Territory north of the Arkansas River by 1863, at least on paper, by their presence at Fort Gibson, with Fort Smith and Fort Scott able to reinforce it in a matter of days. Yet they could do nothing about Stand Watie's raids. His forces roamed at will, always attacking where they were least expected. For two years rumors abounded that he was planning attacks to retake both Fort Smith and Fort Gibson. It was well known that he wanted to bring his people back to their homes, and the Union troops were sitting right smack in the middle of his tribe's land. The Indian Rebels weren't ever able to retake those forts or run their enemy out of Indian Territory. Nonetheless, they did tie up valuable Union manpower and funds that would have been welcomed back East. Stand Watie was truly a thorn in the Union's side.

Getting federal supplies to the soldiers and several thousand Union-sympathizing Indian refugees at Fort Gibson was a challenge, to say the least. After Stand Watie's capture of the steamboat in 1864 and low river levels that summer, the only means of resupply was the overland route from Fort Scott,

Kansas. On September 12 of that year, Major Henry Hopkins of the 2nd Kansas Cavalry started south for Fort Gibson with a heavily laden wagon train. He had over 300 wagons with him with an estimated value at the time of $1.5 million. He had command of 260 regular troops and was reinforced by 100 Union Cherokees along the way.

Major Hopkins suspected that an attempt would be made to take his supply train, and rumors abounded that Confederate General Sterling Price was coming from the east to intercept them. Major Hopkins also suspected that Stand Watie's Indian brigade would raid into the area around Fort Gibson in an attempt to create a diversion while Price's forces set up a large-scale attack. He was only half-right. Stand Watie was coming north, but not as a diversionary force. He had 800 warriors with him and was traveling in force with 1,200 Texas cavalry and artillery troops under General Richard M. Gano.

On September 16, this combined Confederate force reached a point fifteen miles northwest of a manned Union station at Cabin Creek along the route to Fort Gibson. They wanted to sneak through the region until they could locate the supply train, but came upon a crew of Union haycutters at work on a prairie near Flat Rock Creek. Union pickets reported to their officers that they had encountered Confederate troops stealthily approaching their position. Captain E. A. Barker of the 2nd Kansas Cavalry mistook the 200 miscellaneous Texan and Cherokee scouts as the entire force. He led his small group of cavalry troops and a tiny detachment of the 1st Kansas Colored Infantry to meet them before they could go farther and harass the supply train. Captain Barker soon came to realize that he had sadly underestimated the Confederate numbers. The fight quickly went against him, and he dismounted his men in a brushy ravine as the entire Rebel force enveloped them. For half an hour, Barker's men held their position under heavy fire, and things looked dour for them. They were totally surrounded and being picked off like turkeys on a roost. The Texans shouted their awful Rebel yells among the gunfire, and the Cherokee warriors slipped like ghosts through the brush and black-powder smoke, gobbling their wild turkey war cries.

Among the troops in that pitifully outnumbered Union detachment were two Arkansas boys named Cogburn. Captain Barker saw that his men were doomed and ordered all of his cavalry troops to their horses. Those who could were to make a break for another station on Cabin Creek where the wagon train and its large escort were readying for battle. It was every man for himself, and many of their mounts had been killed or were wounded and thrashing pitifully on their sides in the bottom of the ravine. Only sixty-five of Barker's men were able to mount and make a desperate charge through enemy lines toward Cabin Creek. Of those men, only fifteen managed to break through. The unfortunate were captured or killed. One hundred Union troops died, and their officers' reports claimed that the Texas cavalry slaughtered many of the African American soldiers who tried to surrender in the ravine.[46] The Battle of Flat Rock was a complete Confederate success, and close to a massacre. It is uncertain whether John Wesley and Page found horses to try to flee, or had to continue their stand in the ravine. What is certain is that they soon found themselves prisoners of war.

Two days later, Generals Stand Watie and Gano came upon the supply train at the station on Cabin Creek and captured it after a second, larger battle. Union reinforcements were marching northwest from Fort Smith and from nearby Fort Gibson. Much of the supply train had been demolished under heavy cannon fire, but the Confederates still had over 130 intact wagons, 740 mules, and more loot than they could carry back to Texas. The goods were too important to risk losing in another fight, and they fled south, dodging the Union expeditions frantically hunting them. They took their prisoners with them, John Wesley and Page included.

Details of the two men's ordeal on the long journey to Texas are unknown, but they were turned over to the POW camp at Tyler, Texas. Camp Ford was the largest such prison west of the Mississippi. Named in honor of Colonel Rip Ford, the legendary Texas Ranger, the camp consisted of a wooden stockade enclosing a few acres. Prisoners built their own accommodations over the years from logs and whatever other scrap materials they could lay hands on. A stream ran through one edge of the camp, providing water, but it was also a source of disease as it became contaminated by the dense population inside the stockade.

Despite the crude-looking accommodations, Camp Ford's prisoners in the early years lived without too much hardship. But during 1864, the prisoners' numbers tripled and living conditions became horrible, even though the compound size was doubled. Men like John Wesley and Page suffered from lack of food, shelter, clothing, and proper medical attention. Much has been made of Andersonville's deplorable conditions, but as the South became hard-pressed financially to continue the war, Camp Ford was not much better. The standard daily ration of a pint of meal and a pound of beef per prisoner was often not met. Overcrowding and a lack of timber or lumber forced many inmates to live under brush arbors and blanket tents. During the winter, many of the least fortunate, sometimes barefoot and clothed in little more than rags, resorted to digging holes to try to shelter themselves from the cold.

In contrast to the bitter cold of winter, the summer heat in East Texas soared above 100 degrees, and the humidity milked the already weakened prisoners. Page had to watch as his brother became emaciated and wracked by what appeared to be pneumonia, or what John Wesley called "the gravel" in his lungs.

Fevers wracked his body, and strangely, his right ankle became swollen and painful. By the time the South surrendered and a prisoner exchange was arranged, it didn't look as if John Wesley could survive the long trip home.

But he did. He and Page were released from prison on May 22, 1865. There was a family story that Page had managed to hide a single gold piece the whole time they were imprisoned, and he purchased a worn-out plow mule, a decent meal, and a pair of shoes for John Wesley somewhere in Texas. Outfitted thus, they started home with John Wesley riding bareback and Page leading the mule. Wanting to dodge the swamps and river bottoms of the Big Thicket, they wandered north across the Red River into the Choctaw Nation. Somewhere in one of the mountain valleys leading east into Arkansas they were set upon by bandits. The roads and the trails of the time were heavy with such riffraff. Unarmed, the brothers took shelter in some rocky bluffs. They saved themselves with some active ducking and dodging, but lost the mule and one of John Wesley's new shoes. The highwaymen got their mule, and during their frantic escape from the robbers, a crevice in the rocks stole the shoe. Sometime later, they arrived back among their family in rags, as hungry as a she wolf with pups, the weariness of the long miles plain upon them.

However, the family story doesn't exactly match the available evidence. John Wesley's service documents indicate the two Cogburns mustered out, or were released from Union military service, at Fort Leavenworth, Kansas, in September of 1865. According to the testimony of Thomas Whisenhunt, who was a family friend and fellow captive at Camp Ford, those prisoners belonging to the 2nd Kansas were somehow sent from Camp Ford to Fort Gibson and then on to Fort Leavenworth.[47] He recalled that John Wesley was very sick during their internment at Camp Ford and their subsequent release from Union service in Kansas. However, Whisenhunt's recollection took place in 1892.[48] He was sixty-two years old at the time, and perhaps his memory failed him. Maybe John Wesley and Page had enough of the war and slipped off and avoided having to report for mustering out at Fort Leavenworth. A staff sergeant may have simply checked off their names when informed that they had already headed for home. Whatever the case, the family folklore makes for a much better tale.

Although they had managed to survive Camp Ford and come home, John Wesley was never quite the man he was before he left. He was crippled in limb and eaten inside and out by scrofula, a tubercular infection of the lymph nodes.[49] His young wife, formerly Miss Mary B. "Alyora" White of Georgia, had managed as best she could while he was gone, but his homestead at Fancy Hill was in a sad state. He had started building a little house of his own before leaving for war, but he was no longer physically able to complete it. He and Mary had to continue living with his parents, and his pride was as wounded as his body. Some of the extended family had moved off to Texas and weren't around to aid his lonely wife while he was gone. The ground he had worked so hard to clear was overgrown with weeds and brush. Bill, his baby boy, had learned to talk while he was off to war, and might not have recognized the man his mama told him was his daddy.

Despite Mary's nursing, John Wesley's body never healed. He was a shadow of the strapping young man who had left Montgomery County less than a year earlier. In 1866, he and Mary had one more son whom they named John Franklin, but his disease continued to worsen. Tumor-like masses bubbled out on his neck and his right leg. That same limb seemed to atrophy and shriveled away to nothing. The mercury in many of the medicines and poultices doctors placed on his tumors caused his gums to swell and his teeth to loosen in their sockets, as well as making him nauseous and unable to eat at times. The local doctor advised amputating the afflicted leg, but John Wesley refused the operation. Along with the crippling of his body, his lungs and heart began to fail, as if he had never been able to shed the pneumonia that had plagued him while he was a prisoner at Camp Ford. Shortly afterward, in 1868, John Wesley died, leaving his family alone to survive the poverty that was the aftermath of the war.

William Isaac, known as Bill, was only four, and neither he nor Franklin really got to know their father before he was gone. The war had torn apart what little economic structure Montgomery County had possessed before the war, and Reconstruction wouldn't make things any better. The next several years in Arkansas, as in much of the South, were dirty, violent, hard times. It was out of the shambles of war and hardship that John Franklin Cogburn was born—fatherless, destitute, and knowing nothing but trouble.

In 1870, Mary Cogburn married Carter Markham, an Arkansawyer by way of Alabama, and quite a character. Folks who knew him claimed that he was married four times and hung twice in his lifetime. He supposedly bore rope scars around his neck, having been strung up once by Union soldiers and a second time by bushwhackers. U.S. census info doesn't show four wives, associating him with a mere three, and a veritable herd of children. Somewhere along the way he found the time to preach the gospel to mountain folk.

Carter moved Mary north to Sebastian County upon their marriage. For one reason or another, Franklin and Bill were left behind with Nancy, Mary's sister, and her husband William Owensby. Her separation from her young sons was finalized when she passed away in 1873, possibly giving up the ghost during childbirth.[50] There are hints that Mary was already in ill health herself and perhaps had gotten some disease from John Wesley. Neither her nor John Wesley's gravesites are known to the family, but Carter stated in a war pension application for her sons that his brother, Curly, built her a coffin and he buried her himself.[51] The mountains of Arkansas are littered with such lonely, forgotten graves, often marked by little more than a slab of soft sandstone with names scratched into it with a nail.

Franklin was only seven and Bill eleven at the time of their mother's passing. Truly orphans now, the only stable thing they had to cling to was their extended family. And that family was more than just the Cogburns. While the original three brothers who came to that country, their grandfather included, had sired many offspring, the clan was much larger than that. Those who married into the family, and that was most of the neighbors, were also part of the clan—Porters, Whisenhunts, Waggoners, Pates, and many more. If you messed with one of the Cogburns, you had trouble with them all.

Franklin seems to have always been a little too brave and daring for his own good, even as a boy. The clan used to tell how Franklin once brought home two big bear cubs. For want of better equipment, he tied a vine around each of the captured cub's neck and led them like dogs. Either the cubs had been orphaned, or he was simply bold enough to steal them away from their mother. However he caught them, it took him all day to get them home. He would tie one of the cubs up while he dragged the other one along, bawling and squalling and digging its heels in. He would go a ways, tie it up to a tree, and go back for the one he'd left behind. He would then lead it past the one he'd tied and repeat the process. In this leapfrog fashion he slowly made his way home. Despite his rigorous effort and impressive capture, his family wasn't as pleased as he thought they would be. They scolded him for being so foolish as to tangle with a sow's young'uns and immediately loaded the cubs in the back of a wagon and took them back close to where he had captured them. They were afraid that the mother bear would trail her cubs and show up on their doorstep in a very, very bad mood.

By June 1880, fourteen-year-old Franklin was living with his grandfather Patrick and grandmother Elizabeth and working the farm alongside his uncle Mike and three spinster aunts.[52] Sixteen-year-old Bill had gone to live with the Perrin family on Polk Creek near Black Springs, and in September he married Jane Perrin and started a family of his own.

Franklin, on the other hand, wasn't settling down, and he was too young to marry. His uncle Page took him under his wing, but the mixed-up young man grew even wilder. A family letter from one of Franklin's spinster aunts, Martha, states that Franklin was slacking off and not attending to his work. She also states,

> Page makes a big deal out of Franklin and has taken to calling him Rooster on account of how tough he [Franklin] thinks he is. You know as well as I do that it will come to no good if that continues. Page keeps hard company and loves whiskey too much. We all pray that Franklin will come to his senses, but I am afraid that is between him and the Lord. Pray for him like I know you are.[53]

From Page, Franklin learned to tote a rifle like it was a natural part of him, and to hit what he aimed at. In mountain parlance, he could "knock a dime out of a goat's ass" at a hundred yards with his Winchester. He learned every hollow and pass in the mountains, and every ford and crossing on the many rivers and creeks. Page showed him how to ride by night, as the guerrilla fighters on both sides had during the war, and the many tricks to leave pursuit behind or travel without being seen. Franklin learned to make whiskey, a technique and a variety that made a Cogburn batch of mountain dew go down as smooth as a baby's butt and kick like a Missouri mule when it hit bottom. Above all, Franklin was taught that a man's pride and family mattered more than money, and anyone who stepped on either one should be dealt with quickly and without mercy.

Page, upon returning from Camp Ford, took a wife and soon had a growing family. Although older, he was still the restless, bold man he had been when he and Franklin's father marched off to war. Many of the folks in those parts made whiskey for a little something to sip or for jingling money in their pockets, but Page wanted to make more than a little money. By the middle 1880s he had talked others in the clan into joining his venture. The scale of moonshining grew exponentially. Franklin, Bill, their maternal uncle William Owensby, Nathan Owensby, John Barnett, Charlie Johnson, John Porter, Joseph Peppers, John Hollifield, and several other Cogburns ran scattered stills along hidden springs and clear water branches throughout the mountains of southwestern Montgomery County and neighboring Polk and Pike Counties. None of them called Page "Mister," but he was without a doubt the bull of the woods in the operation.

Franklin and Bill Cogburn showed promise that they would grow into strapping men. In an era where most adult men were much shorter, Bill was six foot four in his prime, and Franklin was six foot one. Both of them were much taller than most of their kin, but they were still basically just kids, and Page needed a lieutenant he could trust. Whiskey meant money, and with so many bad men and desperate men wandering the countryside, many a still or cache was stolen or load hijacked. The clan structure of the mountain families led to more than one feud, and every one of those families had a salty man or two to handle any rough business.

James Lafayette Cogburn was a first cousin to Page. He was the son of James Cogburn, who was the first of the Cogburns to come to Fancy Hill. Lafayette was a popular name of the time, and mountain folk pronounced it "Fate." Fayette was born in 1842 and was a Union infantry veteran. All the Cogburns shared the glassy, dark, Indian eyes, but his were so piercing as to almost shine. Meeting his gaze was like looking into the eyes of a panther about to pounce. Fayette was only five feet eight, but his temper was as hot as the August sun, and it was a trait he and Franklin shared.[54] He'd charge hell with a bucket of water if his mad was up.

By the time Deputy Marshal Trammell came to live at Fancy Hill among the Cogburns, the whiskey operation was booming. There was little industry beyond a few small sawmills and gristmills in the county. Most folks made or bartered for what they needed, and any kind of coin was hard to come by. Moonshining was the best source of income for many of the mountain folk. A corn patch might feed a family, but it wouldn't buy the kids shoes and the wife a bolt of dress material. However, a bushel of corn turned into whiskey was a whole different story. Many men of the time were drinkers, and good moonshine was the same as liquid cash. The bars and saloons in Hot Springs, Little Rock, and every picnic grounds and settlement for miles provided a ready market for their goods.

Moonshiners and American bourbon distillers will tell you to this day that it takes clear mountain water to make good whiskey. Accordingly, mountainous frontier Arkansas had as much whiskey as it had water. There is the old, often told folktale poking fun at the popularity of 'shine in the state, especially among backwoodsmen. In this tale, an Arkansas settler bought five gallons of moonshine from a peddler or a merchant. He returned one week later for more sippin' liquor, and the man who sold him the product was thoroughly amazed.

"Surely you ain't drunk all that whiskey already?" the seller asked.

"It weren't so much," replied the backwoods farmer. "There's six of us counting the wife and kids, and we ain't got no milk cow at all."[55]

While the tale might be stretching things a bit, there is some truth in it. And Arkansas wasn't the only place a moonshiner could sell his product. Whiskey brought an even higher premium in the Indian Nations to the west if a man was bold and savvy enough to haul it in under the noses of Judge Parker's continually prowling marshals. A gallon of whiskey might fetch as much as ten dollars there. In accordance with such extravagant prices, the fines if a bootlegger was caught in the Nations were more than double those in the States. A whiskey peddler was also much more likely to be sentenced to jail if caught there, but for many, the temptation of a ready market was too much to resist.

The booze made within Indian Territory was in no way enough to meet the demand there. It was outlaw country, and without the necessary liquor to properly impair judgment, half of the exciting, derring-do gunfights and wild times would never have happened. Dime novels and Western pulp have always portrayed gunfights fought over notions of honor or the affections of beautiful ladies of the night. But in truth, liquor had more to do with the violence than any of that romantic-sounding stuff ever did. Frontier-made whiskey went by several monikers, such as "rattlesnake venom," "panther piss," "brown mule," and "white lightning." In addition to its relaxing qualities, it could be used to strip paint, disinfect wounds, or start a fire. There was a good reason why the court charges often labeled whiskey as "spirituous liquors." Such whiskey as made by the Cogburns could definitely put spirit in a drinker. Given ample doses of such distillations, mild men might find themselves ready to wrestle a tiger. After consuming enough liquid bravery, a simple railway worker or coal miner might turn into the tall, broad-shouldered, narrow-hipped, two-gun badass of the shoot-'em-up Western novel. How boring would it have been for two pistol-packing desperadoes to bump into each other in a saloon and soberly contemplate the consequences and politely apologize to each other? A little whiskey ensured that they might drunkenly pull their smoke poles and burn friction at each other until one or both of them bled.

And those dance hall girls? Single, eligible females of any kind could be hard to find in the Nations. The kind of women that hung around Indian Territory taverns and whiskey tents weren't likely to win any beauty pageants. Some of the prostitutes were dope fiends, and the years of long nights, tobacco smoke, whiskey, and miles of hard living behind them had taken any beauty they might have once possessed. The good-looking soiled doves could make a fortune in the fancy bordellos along the river in Fort Smith. The frontier dives were usually the last resting place of women too used up, too mean, or too ugly for the gilded wallpaper and feather beds of the high-toned cathouses such as Miss Laura's Social Club. Only a drunken man would fight over some of the hags in the Nations.

To meet the demand for spirits in the Nations, whiskey peddlers hauled their product across the border by the gallon in wagons and packsaddles. And the booze wasn't always smuggled in such great volumes. Many a traveler stashed a single bottle of John Barleycorn in their suitcase or hid it in their bedroll. Women were known to hide hooch in their dresses, where the morality and reserve of the Victorian-era marshals was supposed to prevent them from searching. Even if these small-scale smugglers were teetotalers, there were plenty of drinkers willing to buy what they could manage to bring with them. The sale of such might pay their stagecoach fare or train ticket.

Whiskey making, especially bootlegging into the Nations, was so profitable that Judge Parker's jurisdiction was overrun by moonshiners and whiskey peddlers willing to risk his wrath. This was especially true in the southwest corner of Arkansas—

Cogburn country. Pike County, joining Montgomery County to the south, had its own moonshining gang. A *New York Times* article from 1889 gives an idea of the scale of some of the illegal distillery operations:

NOTED MOONSHINERS CAPTURED

Little Rock, Arkansas, June 3—Deputy United States Marshal Faulkenberry arrived here from Pike County having in charge H. Faulkner and J. M. Horton, two of the most noted moonshiners in the state and leaders of a notorious gang of desperadoes.

A number of unsuccessful efforts have been made and many lives lost in the attempt to capture this gang. The still-house was found in first-class order, with a capacity of 130 gallons per day. Nearly two thousand gallons of mash and a quantity of whiskey were also captured.[56]

And moonshiners were no less desperate in their attempts to resist arrest than were the train robbers, murderers, and highwaymen plaguing the countryside. Heck Thomas, possibly the most famous of the deputy marshals riding for the Hanging Judge and the survivor of many a gunfight and dangerous encounter, came as close to dying by gunshot as he ever did while trying to arrest the Purdy Gang along Snake Creek, Indian Territory. The gang had built a log-and-stone wall across a deep ravine, and Thomas boldly led his posse up to the barricade and demanded surrender. The moonshiners immediately opened fire, hitting Thomas twice and knocking him from his saddle.[57] Armed, violent men sitting around a still dripping out whiskey were liable to make reckless decisions when it came to the sudden appearance of lawmen near their "makings." Shooting first and asking questions later could be preferable to spending time in prison. Arresting moonshiners was clearly a job for brave men, and a risky venture at best.

As early as 1886, names of the Cogburn clan began showing up on Judge Parker's dockets. They were caught either making whiskey or selling it, but little came of the charges. The Hanging Judge could threaten all the fines or jail time he wanted, but that wasn't going to stop their operations. By 1888, that fierce old judge and the U.S. Marshal's office had decided that no matter what, they were going to do just that. Things had gotten out of hand. Franklin Cogburn's attempt to hunt down Deputy Marshal Trammell and kill him was the straw that broke the camel's back. It was time the moonshiner gangs were broken up once and for all; those outlaws needed to be taught a little respect for the law.

But the Hanging Judge had to catch and arrest the Cogburns first, and that was much easier said than done, at least until J. D. Trammell came to Fancy Hill and did his detective work. The court had the evidence it needed and was only lacking the culprits. It was time for war on the moonshiners, and war it was to be. Neither the deputy marshals nor the Cogburns would have it any other way.

5

Vengeance and Lead

Deputy Marshal J. D. Trammell was obviously the nervy man many said he was. Like an old-time Texas cattle buyer once liked to say, he had more guts than a slaughterhouse. His undercover work against the Cogburns was more than enough to prove his courage, but he was about to be tested again. According to his daughter Lucetta, the Cogburns left a note nailed to his door after he had arrived back at his home near Huntington, Arkansas, that read, *If you come back we'll kill you.*[58] Apparently, he wasn't one to be bullied or cowed. It wasn't long after this that he and the posse headed south to Montgomery County to arrest the Cogburn moonshiners. He had shaken up a hornet's nest and was riding right back into the swarm.

Trammell was obviously in the right, as far as the law was concerned. He was apparently a clean-cut man who owned a fine, large log home and had accumulated a small herd of cattle. His children adored him, and he supported and sheltered his blind mother, who served as a caretaker for his children after the death of his second wife in 1884. But many Cogburns also claimed that he, along with several other of the deputies in the posse, were Confederate veterans and ill-disposed toward the Mountain Federals like the Cogburns. If true, that just added more kerosene to an already burning fire. And when the posse raided the first of the clan's whiskey stills and arrested Bill Cogburn, the deputy marshals might as well have fanned the flames with the brims of their big hats.

The other three men arrested were released for lack of evidence, having just been caught in the area of the stills, but Bill Cogburn and Joseph Peppers were held in camp to be hauled back to Fort Smith. News can travel surprisingly fast, even in the rough and steep mountains, and the clan at Fancy Hill soon knew what had happened. Five men gathered their rifles and filled their pockets with ammunition. Franklin Cogburn and his cousin Fayette were dead set on freeing Bill. Franklin must have decided he could rescue his brother and finally deal with Trammell all at once.

Miles away, the posse camped for the night, and on the following morning, June 26, 1888, discussed where they should raid next. Trammell quickly stated that he was going to Fancy Hill to smoke out Franklin and Fayette Cogburn. Many of the marshals pointed out that such actions would be a good way to get killed. There were nothing but Cogburns down that way, and nobody in his right mind had any doubt how a marshal would be greeted by them when on the prod. Trammell was insistent, and deputy marshals Reuben Fry and Otis Wheeler finally agreed to patrol the roads near Fancy Hill and see who they could run across. Little did they know that the Cogburns were up in arms and riding to meet them. And leading five tougher-than-nails hill boys was twenty-two-year-old Franklin "Rooster" Cogburn.

Sometime that morning, while the three deputy marshals were passing through heavy timber along the trail from Black Springs to Fancy Hill, Trammell got a little bit ahead of the other two. He came to a crossroads where the trail forked one way to Caddy Gap and the other to Fancy Hill. Trammell looked up the road and saw Franklin and his cohorts coming his way with fight on their minds and armed to the teeth. It has been lost to history, but perhaps Franklin and J. D. Trammell were the only people ever to know which one of them saw the other first. Both men knew that a killing was inevitable the next time they ran across each other, and neither man was going to back down. On that June early morning, with the rising sun filtering down through the pine timber on that lonely mountain road, and the crows circling and cawing as they came off their roosts, the time was finally at hand for a reckoning.

Trammell stopped in the intersection and turned his head to yell back to the other deputies. "Look out, here they come!"[59]

As soon as the words left Trammell's mouth, a rifle shot rang out. According to later testimony by the lawmen, there were four other men with Franklin coming down the road to meet the deputies. The Cogburns would later claim that Trammell either attempted to raise his rifle or went for the short gun at his hip when he laid eyes on his enemies. The court records and newspaper articles are sadly lacking in details, and Deputy Reuben Fry's various newspaper testimonies give very little more.

The *Fort Smith Elevator*, after interviewing Deputy Fry, stated the Winchester bullet struck Trammell "squarely in the breast" and he "fell from his horse dead."[60] Deputies Fry and Wheeler immediately dismounted and took cover in the brush to the side of the road, ready to defend themselves. One other shot was fired in the direction of the deputies, and then their attackers retreated. The officers only got glimpses of them filtering through the timber.

Sometime later, some women who lived nearby were convinced to watch over Trammell's body while the surviving deputy marshals rode to Black Springs to report the shooting. A coroner's jury was summoned to hold an inquest at the scene. It was ascertained that two of the murderers were relatives of the posse's prisoner, Bill Cogburn—Franklin and their cousin Fayette. The other three men were later identified as Nathan Owensby, John Barnett, and Charles (Charlie) Johnson.[61]

Trammell's body was moved to Black Springs, and the posse quickly relocated there for fear of the Cogburns coming in force to try to rescue Bill. The locals were questioned at length as to the identities of the men who had attacked the deputy marshals and shot Trammell, but apparently many of them either sided with the Cogburns or feared crossing them too much to talk. Deputy Reuben Fry later claimed that some of them were fed up with the Cogburns' outlaw behavior and wanted to help, but he never seemed to get much aid from them. However, Fry did become certain that Franklin and Fayette Cogburn were the two men responsible for killing Trammell.

It was decided that Fry would go to Fort Smith to confer with the U.S. Marshal while the rest of his fellow deputies would stay behind to guard Bill Cogburn. Joseph Pepper was released on his own recognizance. Deputy U.S. Marshals Otis Wheeler, John Strozier , and J. M. Cain were soon wishing they too had gone to Fort Smith. While Fry was at Fort Smith pleading with his superiors for a large force to go back to Montgomery County and arrest Fayette and Franklin Cogburn, the clan was gathering around Black Springs. They were reported to be forty strong, violent, and well armed. Allies, whom the *Fort Smith Elevator* termed as "a gang from nearby Polk County under the leadership of a notorious moonshiner named Brooks," showed up to reinforce the Cogburns.[62] The outnumbered peace officers quickly decided that they had to come up with an escape plan or let Bill Cogburn go.

John Porter, a local and a cousin of the Cogburns, was assisting the deputies along with Montgomery County Sheriff G. W. Golden.[63] They and W. J. "Jack" Hopper, a nearby postmaster and store owner, devised a plan to get the prisoner out of town. The posse's prisoner wagon was abandoned, and Hopper and the four other lawmen slipped away with their prisoner on horseback in the late hours of Saturday night.

Guided by Hopper, the cautious officers avoided the main road and wound their way through the mountains to the county seat at Mount Ida. The town was full of rumors that the Cogburns intended to rescue Bill the next night and that every road and trail out of the area was well guarded to prevent the officers' escape. With the addition of a few more county deputies, the prisoner was guarded throughout the day until the Deputy U.S. Marshals could sneak off with him once again in the night. They kept to the brush and managed to reach Crystal Springs by Monday morning. They rested their horses until noon before proceeding on to Hot Springs. Porter and Wheeler loaded Bill Cogburn onto a train bound for Fort Smith while the other deputies stayed behind in the city with the horses to await the reinforcements they thought Deputy Fry was sure to bring.

Reuben Fry had little luck in convincing his superiors to grant him a small army to smoke out the Cogburns. Perhaps this is why he pleads so in various newspaper articles. According to him, "[he] will probably have to abandon the idea of bringing the parties [Cogburns] to justice, as he [Fry] cannot get the force necessary to cope with them."[64]

Fry also claimed that Jack Hopper, who had been left behind at Mount Ida, was to be killed by the Cogburns for aiding the lawmen in getting Bill Cogburn out of the county. He even went so far as to assert that Hopper was most certainly already dead at the Cogburns' hands by the time of his reporting.[65] In fact, Jack Hopper was safe and sound. During his pandering to the public for aid in his quest for revenge against the Cogburns, Fry was unaware that Hopper and Fayette Cogburn had served together in the 1st Arkansas Union Infantry. Some sense of justice must have driven Hopper to aid the deputy marshals, but he and the Cogburns had always been on good terms. They traded at his store often and shared the common bond of being Mountain Federals. While it is certain the Cogburns didn't like him aiding the lawmen, perhaps he could be excused as not having participated in the original raid on the moonshiners and subsequent shoot-out. For whatever reason, he went unscathed.

For the moment, J. D. Trammell was the only victim of the Cogburns. Trammell family lore has it that some of the posse eventually rode into the yard of the deceased deputy marshal's home at Huntington. Trammell's blind mother, Mary, was sitting on the porch when they arrived. Sightless though she was, perhaps she sensed the bad news coming in the quiet approach of the lawmen and the serious, uncertain tone of their voices. Her grandchildren may have watched from behind her with big eyes, knowing also that something had gone terribly wrong for their father. The somber lawmen and bearers of bad news were leading Trammell's horse with its empty saddle and his guns strapped on it. They dropped the horse's bridle reins and said, "Mrs. Trammell, your son was killed and we buried him."[66] His body was supposedly interred at a cemetery in Black Springs, but no tombstone remains. His descendants searched for his grave in later years, but the location of his mortal remains has been lost to time. As many of the Cogburns lived at Caddo Cove, the earlier community very near to Black Springs, it is possible that he was buried in that vicinity in a forgotten graveyard.[67] The cemetery at Mount Gilead Baptist Church contains the graves of many who perished in those years, but there is no tombstone there bearing his name. Perhaps the fallen peace officer never even got a marker for his six feet of cold, hard ground.

Franklin and Fayette Cogburn, along with their three supposed accomplices, were now wanted men. By July 20, 1888, the U.S. Marshal had placed a $200-per-man bounty on their heads, plus an additional $300 added by the Arkansas Governor's Office. The wanted notice for Trammell's killers was posted in the July 13, 1888, *Fort Smith Elevator* and subsequent editions in the following two weeks.

Hollywood has often shown wanted posters nailed to sheriff's offices listing bounties worth a prince's ransom for the apprehension of desperadoes along with lithographed depictions of their faces. In truth, early wanted notices rarely showed a portrait of the fugitive and were usually posted in newspapers rather than mailed out to various law enforcement offices. Five hundred dollars was a large sum for the time, unless the wanted men were bank or train robbers with private express or railroad company bonuses increasing the bounty. The amount offered for J. D. Trammell's murderers was more than enough to motivate any number of freelance bounty hunters. It would also bring more Deputy U.S. Marshals onto the scene with the possibility of increasing their meager pay. The federal lawmen weren't always eligible for government bounties, but it wouldn't hurt to try.[68]

Such a price on his head could tempt friends into turning on a wanted man and make him wonder who he could trust. It would seem that Franklin's only chance was to run away from Arkansas into the Nations, or elsewhere, far from the Hanging Judge's long arm. But that was not to be. Franklin and the other four men wanted for Trammell's murder weren't going anywhere. All of them denied having pulled the trigger, at least to the Law, but to a man they felt that the lawman had gotten what he deserved. They saw Trammell as a sneaky traitor, a woman beater, and a corrupt deputy with a personal prejudice against Union veterans. Montgomery County was their home, and they refused to flee. The Hanging Judge and all his gunmen could go straight to the Devil.

6

The Slow Wheels of Justice

With the considerable reward offered and lawmen scouring the brush, it would seem inevitable that the five men wanted for Trammell's murder would be caught. Much like today, the death of a fellow peace officer had every lawman in the area out for blood, and Franklin and his friends were marked men. But the terrain of Montgomery County lent itself well to hiding fugitives, and it didn't seem that any of the five outlaws would be bound over for justice unless they wanted to be. Strangely, that is just what happened.

As has been said earlier, the $500 dollar reward per man sounded like a pot of gold at the end of the rainbow to the poor folk of Montgomery County. A man didn't make his living in the mountains by his strong back alone. Wits are what separate humans from the beasts, and Arkansas had more than its share of crafty, wily citizens. The dumb folks down that way had already starved out and gone elsewhere. The clan was confident in their numbers and in their isolation from the rest of the world. If the government was fool enough to offer such a reward, then they wouldn't look a gift horse in the mouth.

Sometime in late July, it was rumored that a grand jury was going to indict all five suspects for first degree murder. Franklin and his friends showed up at Mount Ida and turned themselves in. It may be going a little far to claim that they actually handed themselves over to the Law, as none of them were willing to relinquish their firearms. They did have a supposed captor along with each of them, and a large group of heavily armed male members of the clan followed in their wake. The court could hear their case and then pay those who had brought them. Franklin and his friends were sure that they would go home free, and $2,500 richer for their audacity.

Onto the scene walked Deputy U.S. Marshal Dave Vancel Rusk, all five feet four of him. Rusk made up for his pint-sized stature with courage that would have overflowed a fifty-five-gallon barrel. The little storekeeper and lawman was apparently far tougher than he appeared. He had ridden as a Confederate cavalryman during the war and was as tenacious as a bulldog in pursuing outlaws. During the late 1880s and early 1890s, he participated in four gun battles between lawmen and Ned Christie before that famous Cherokee outlaw was finally blasted from his fort with dynamite and cannon. Rusk would help avenge the murder of another deputy marshal in January of 1889 when he led a posse that shot to death the desperado Wesley Barnett.[69]

J. D. Trammell's and Reuben Fry's whiskey investigation and raid had revealed the identities of many of the Cogburns involved in moonshining. Affidavits accusing Franklin, Page, Fayette, Bill, and many others of illegal whiskey operations from 1887 to early 1888 were signed by Fry in July, just after the shooting at Fancy Hill.[70] Trammell's death had the marshal's office in an uproar, and nothing was going to satisfy the lawmen until the culprits were brought to justice. Plans were made to clean out Montgomery County once and for all. Dave

Rusk was sent down there to subpoena and round up witnesses.

The *Fort Smith Elevator* of August 3 had this to say about Rusk's success in this endeavor, and the Cogburns turning themselves over to the Law:

> Deputy Dave Rusk came in from Montgomery County Monday with Carter Markham, Matthew Pervine, and Joseph Pepper, attached witnesses in the Cogburn moonshine whiskey case, and J. D. Hollifield, a Montgomery County farmer, charged with selling moonshine whiskey. Mr. Rusk says the five men who participated in the murder of Deputy U.S. Marshal Trammell have all been arrested and released by a magistrate, as no witnesses appeared against them, and no one was present to prosecute. Their examination was a mere farce, and during its progress they were surrounded by their friends all well armed, who would have released them had they been bound over. Rusk had writs for all of them on charges of illicit distilling but did not go to the trial, as the sheriff had warned him that it would be extremely dangerous, as he would likely be killed. He then requested the sheriff to turn over to him Fayette and Franklin Cogburn, two of the alleged murderers, whom he has in custody, and assist him in getting them out of the country. The sheriff sent him word that he could not get a force large enough to take them out, as it would be impossible, and they were released. The reward of $300 offered by the governor for the murderers has been withdrawn and the question now arises, can the parties who

arrested them collect the reward offered by the government [U.S. Marshal's Office]—$200 each. The four men brought in by Rusk were taken before Commissioner Wheeler Tuesday, but their examination was continued to await the summoning of more witnesses.

The Cogburns thumbing their noses at the court went off without a hitch, except for the government reneging on the promised rewards. Not one cent of the governor's bounty or the one promised by the U.S. Marshals was ever paid to the five wanted men's fake captors. Franklin and his friends went back to their mountain strongholds no richer, but the Hanging Judge's lawmen were unable to stop them.

If Trammell's killers were still running free, it wasn't because the Law wasn't working hard to bring them to justice. An arrest warrant was issued for Page Cogburn on whiskey charges in an attempt to stomp the head of the snake that the lawmen saw as the entire Cogburn clan. Page agreed to meet Rusk on neutral ground at Waldron, where he turned himself over on August 11. There was nothing to be gained by trying to avoid capture when only a fine could be expected for a first conviction.

Soon after Page's arrest, on August 24, the Law turned the heat up on Franklin a little more. Another grand jury was convened and first degree murder indictments were handed down for all five of the men present the day Trammell was killed. In part, it reads as follows:

Fayette Cogburn, Franklin Cogburn, Nath. Owensby, John Barnett, and Charlie Johnson then and there held in their hands loaded with gunpowder and leaden bullets . . . to kill and mur-

der [Trammell] against the peace and dignity of
the state of Arkansas.[71]

Fayette and Bill Cogburn, Nathan Owensby, Charlie Johnson, and John Barnett were also indicted for whiskey crimes in
an attempt to pile on the stack of charges against the clan and
break up the moonshining gang once and for all. The Hanging
Judge's men now had what they needed to really go after those
they wanted so badly. Franklin and the rest were truly at war
with the court at Fort Smith.

If the deputy marshals thought the Cogburns were going to
fold up and surrender, they were sadly mistaken. Franklin,
Fayette, and their crew began building breastworks and rifle
pits on high positions near their homes and sleeping out in the
brush if their many lookouts warned them of lawman or
strangers nearby. Stubbornly, they still moved about the settlements and tended their farms, but they did so in force and kept
their horses near at hand. Not only did they not intend to run
away from Montgomery County, they were digging in.

Before the age of mass transit, modern communications,
driver's licenses, and Social Security numbers, locating witnesses and summoning them could be a lengthy and difficult
task. Deputy marshals logged long hours and hundreds of miles
serving subpoenas for fees and mileage. The court subpoenas
threatened the desired witnesses with stiff fines and the power
of the United States for failure to appear. But even when found
and served, those witnesses might move to unknown parts and
the legal process could be delayed and hearings and trials
rescheduled. Many a charged criminal went free in those days
when he could avoid the Law long enough either for witnesses
to disappear or for their memories to fade. Every day a criminal
could remain out of court, the greater the chances were of being
found innocent by a jury due to lack of evidence. Franklin and
his allies were going to wait it out or fight it out.

While there is nothing in the surviving newspaper articles that tells of the last months of 1888 for these cases, family tales abound. There are vague and jumbled stories of deputies being fired upon from the brush when scouting around the Cogburns and attempting to subpoena or question witnesses—hats shot off and creased and other near misses. By the fall, the peace officers' attempts seemed to have slackened, and unserved writs of arrest lay on the Fort Smith prosecutor's desk. Cogburn country did seem to be pure poison for lawmen.

However, cracks began to show in the hard shell of the clan. There were those in the communities of Black Springs, Caddo Gap, and the settlement at Fancy Hill who felt the moonshining and lawlessness had gone too far. Franklin and his friends were bringing undue attention to the area. Many a family who had past disagreements with one or more of the clan saw a chance to get even by giving peace officers information. With the roughest of the Cogburns "on the scout" and making rarer appearances in town, many of their dissenters became bold enough to voice their complaints.

It wasn't only those outside the clan beginning to voice their opinions, but some inside as well. There were those who had come to like Trammell while he lived among them and thought his killing was a sad, sorry affair. Furthermore, some of those in-laws, cousins, and friends who weren't sorry to see Trammell dead also weren't as keen on fighting it out with the Law as Franklin and Fayette seemed to be. In addition, some of those indicted for making moonshine may have seen a chance to give state's evidence against Franklin and Fayette in exchange for amnesty. Joseph Peppers and John Hollifield were two of the Cogburn clan suspected of doing so. This lack of unity hurt the wanted men more than the multitude of lawmen against them.

Besides their numbers, the Cogburns' greatest strength had always been the fact that the mountain folk had always seen theirs as a separate world, and anybody from outside the area was considered a foreigner. A Fort Smith badge had always meant as little to a lot of Montgomery County citizens as somebody showing up with a crown on his head and proclaiming to be the King of France. The mountain folk felt they were more than capable of handling troubles among themselves. Unless a man had done something heinous such as rape, he could usually count on his neighbors to give any peace officer the cold shoulder. That same neighbor might even send runners out to warn the wanted man after that lawman left. Mountain folk had always looked after their own, but the times were changing.

In the late summer and fall of 1888, rumors abounded about who was selling out the moonshiners. Many a false warning was given during the middle of the night that Parker's boys were nearby and riding to arrest the guilty and accused. Not knowing who might stab him in the back, Franklin turned to those few he could trust—the families of Fayette, Page, and his brother Bill. Franklin's grandfather Patrick counseled peace and caution where the Law was concerned, hoping things would settle down and his grandson would be acquitted of Trammell's death. Fayette's younger brother, Leander, was a firebrand just like Fayette. He kept an eye on the roads in and out of Fancy Hill, and his rifle ready for trouble.

Not all those whose necks were at risk if they went before the Hanging Judge were willing to wait things out and see if the whole deal would be forgotten. With the odds beginning to look in the Law's favor, Nathan Owensby, the brother of Franklin's uncle and one of the five indicted for murder and making whiskey, fled Montgomery County for Indian Territory. The court may have decided he wasn't responsible for Trammell's murder, having only been present as a witness, or simply gave up ever finding him. He was never brought to justice concerning any of the events of 1888. Whatever the case may have been, he came back to Arkansas not many years later. He was arrested for making whiskey in nearby Polk County in 1893, but fled back to Indian Territory once more before his court date. Some of his descendants claim that he was later involved in a gunfight near what is now Stewart, Oklahoma, where he killed a man sometime after 1900.

If secondhand family tales are to be believed, Franklin too went to Indian Territory, but only for a little while. And it wasn't because he wanted to hide from the deputy marshals. An old-time resident of Black Springs once told of waking up in her bed one night to the sound of horses running up and down the street and the excited voices of men gathered by lantern light. A posse of citizens had ridden up the river from Amity in search of some horse thieves who had raided through their settlement. They had lost the outlaws' trail earlier that evening and presumed the stolen livestock was already in the Indian Nations. Many of the residents of Black Springs went to secure their horses and mules in case the vigilantes were wrong about where the outlaws were. All the livestock of the settlement were accounted for and things quieted down after the Amity men rode back south the next morning. Everybody soon forgot about the scare, except for the Cogburns.

The outlaws had stolen a team of mules from Patrick Cogburn on their way west. Franklin, his brother Bill, and Page Cogburn took their rifles down off their porch pegs and saddled their horses to go after the thieves.[72] They found witnesses south of Dallas, Arkansas, who had seen the outlaws pass. They had little luck tracking the bandits, but played a hunch and followed the old wagon trail toward the Choctaw settlement at Lenox, Indian Territory—a long ride west into the Kiamichi River Valley.

A week later, the three Cogburns arrived back home on frazzled horses and acting unusually grim. They had little to say about their manhunt, but they were leading Patrick's stolen mules. According to legend, when a neighbor told Patrick he'd better keep a lookout for thieves in the future, the old man chuckled and told him that the bunch who stole his mules wouldn't be bothering anybody's stock. What he implied but didn't say was that his grandsons and Page had taken care of the bandit problem. Nothing much was ever said about the horse rustlers. The trio of Cogburns who went after them never told where they found them or where they left them lying.

Franklin may have fought outlaws, but he was also one himself. He was wanted by the Law and peace officers were apt to show up anytime to arrest him. Stubbornly, he dug in his heels. He may have been the calm, cool type, or perhaps he was just one of those who didn't give a damn about consequences. Anyway, he continued on with his life, which was changing as rapidly as the coming winter weather. The Hanging Judge and his pack of deputies may have wanted to stretch his neck, but a young man sometimes has more important things to attend to than his health. Pretty, eligible girls could be scarce in those parts, but Franklin found himself one. All he had to do was to keep the Law off his back long enough to court her.

7

The Tennessee Lady

Joseph Spurling came to northwest Arkansas sometime between 1879 and 1880. The gray-eyed Tennessean settled into Benton County in the Ozarks for a time to practice medicine. Sometime later, prior to 1888, he moved his family to Montgomery County.[73] His sister Elzada was the widow of James Cogburn, Fayette's father. Joseph settled down near Black Springs to be close to her and his nieces and nephews.

The troubles of his in-laws might not have even fazed him. A little country spat and shooting affray with some deputy marshals wasn't overwhelming for a man who had seen enough fighting for two lifetimes. He had served with the 43rd Tennessee Infantry, 5th East Tennessee Volunteers, CSA, in the war and was captured at Big Black, Mississippi, during the Confederate defense of Vicksburg in 1863. He wound up in a Union prison camp near Fort Delaware, just outside of Baltimore, Maryland. Possibly he was a prisoner at Point Lookout on the southern tip of the Maryland peninsula.

In 1864, President Abraham Lincoln knew how sick Northerners were of the war drafts and how badly his commanders needed reinforcements to replace the wounded and the deserters resulting from two years of continuous fighting. He heeded the suggestion of Major General Benjamin Butler and gave his blessing to recruiting among the Confederate prisoners to see who might want to swap loyalties. Many of the prisoners were never staunch secessionists, had joined the Confederacy late because of farms and families at home that they worried about, or were war weary and had decided the South could never win. Conditions at Point Lookout, like every other overcrowded POW camp on both sides during the war, were less than wonderful. Butler's staff and prison guards interviewed prisoners and offered them the opportunity to do road work, to fight for the Union, or to go home to their families within Union lines. The prisoners were promised release from their horrible conditions in prison and a pay in Union cash if they decided to join up. Despite the federal government's official policies to the contrary, Butler began releasing prisoners who took an oath not to bear arms against the Union again, or set them free in prisoner exchanges with the South.[74] The Union troops gave the Confederates who swapped allegiance the name "Galvanized Yankees," as their supposed loyalty went no deeper than the blue uniform they donned to get out of lockup.

In July 1863, Joseph was transferred to Virginia in preparation for a prisoner exchange. However, for some reason, he decided to remain where he was and fight for the Union.[75] General Ulysses S. Grant didn't trust the turncoat recruits, but the Sioux Indian outbreak in Minnesota and in the Dakota Territory might be just the place for them. Major General John Pope needed soldiers to man his forts out that way, and sending the Galvanized Yankees to him would keep the critically needed normal Union regiments fighting against the South.

On October 5, 1863, Joseph became a member of G Company, 1st Regiment Connecticut Cavalry as a wagoner and farrier. His regiment performed various duties around Baltimore and Point Lookout, and even made a patrol of the road into Brandywine Station, Virginia. But most commanders didn't have any faith in the Galvanized Yankees' ability or willingness to kill their fellow Southerners. It was Indian fighting that the force was bound for, and on April 26, 1864, the first Galvanized Yankees were sent by riverboat to Fort Snelling, Minnesota (Minneapolis–St. Paul) and then marched to Fort Ridgely by the end of June. The Sioux were raising hell along the frontier and had even attacked Fort Ridgely in the summer of 1862. G Company also saw duty at Fort Ripley, Madelia, and Leavenworth. The troops were undersupplied and the winters were vicious, especially for men who had grown up in the South. Temperatures of thirty degrees below zero insured that a soldier was more apt to be frozen stiff than scalped by the fierce and angry Sioux.[76]

In later years, Joseph would entertain the family with yarns from his soldiering years. He often told the story of a starving, ragged Indian wandering into the fort during one of the cold and awful blizzards of the winter of 1864–65. The poor man wanted food, and all the soldiers had to give him was salt pork. The Indian immediately wolfed down a prodigious amount of the briny meat. Shortly afterward, he was found dead lying beside a nearby stream. The other soldiers assumed that the famished brave had simply eaten himself to death, but Joseph always believed that the large amount of salt used as a preservative in the ration had overwhelmed the Indian's weakened body and killed him. The salt had created a crazy thirst in the Indian, and he was thus found dead by the stream.

The Galvanized Yankees were seen by the government as successful enough in their role as frontier peacekeepers, and more regiments were raised. G Company was reformed as the Independent Company, 1st U.S. Volunteers on April 5, 1865. In the fall of 1865, Joseph took the option of mustering out and went back to east Tennessee.

Finally home, he attended a quilting party. Women of the 1800s had invented a new means of breaking the monotony of the long days of raising families and tending homes. Invitations, usually sent by word of mouth in frontier or rural areas, requested neighbor ladies to attend. The hostess would provide fabric and a quilting frame hung from the ceiling of her home, porch, brush arbor, or even to be set on the seamstresses' knees if other accommodations weren't available. Her friends would bring their sewing needles and expertise.

However, such quiltings or quilting bees were more than just a chance for a few wives of the community to get together and make bed coverings and chitchat. They were a social gathering for both sexes. The event was closely akin to the backyard barbecues or pool parties of today. While the women sewed and caught up on the latest events in their friends' lives, the men pitched horseshoes, talked of crops and politics, and swapped all manner of lies and tall tales. Children ran in and out of the day-long affair, and a noon or evening feast brought everyone together. Musicians among the gathering might strike up a tune, and those who wished would sing or dance. Joseph himself was known as an exceptional fiddle player, and perhaps he rosined up his bow and made the mountains ring with tunes like "Mississippi Sawyer" and "Cumberland Gap."

And quiltings served one other social function. Bachelors were given the chance to visit with eligible maidens, and more than a little courting took place. The 1856 song "Aunt Dinah's Quilting Party," also known as "Seeing Nellie Home," tells of a young man walking a sweetheart back from a quilting.

Apparently, Joseph was a friend of the Sharits family before he went to war. Stephen Sharits, the patriarch, was a successful farmer with twelve children, most of them grown and living nearby. He had emigrated from Virginia to east Tennessee many years earlier, and his family was deeply religious and staunchly pro-Union when the Civil War broke out. Three of his sons served in various Tennessee Union cavalry and mounted infantry regiments. One of the boys was killed in battle in 1862, and a son and son-in-law made it through combat only to suffer a similar fate.

Winton Sharits and John McPhail, Winton's brother-in-law, were both coming home on the paddle-wheel steamship *Sultana* in April of 1865. The ship was overcrowded with troops, many of them just released prisoners of war in very poor physical condition. The boilers exploded and approximately 1,400 men were either burned to death or drowned. Winton Sharits survived by clinging to a chunk of debris, but McPhail perished.

Apparently, another of the sons, Guy Sharits, was a close friend of Joseph Spurling and brought him to the quilting. During the day's festivities, Guy's pretty sister caught Joseph's eye.[77] Sarah Sharits was twenty-two and single, on the verge of being a spinster in those times. He had only a day to talk with her, but he was apparently thinking of her even after he left the state to find work and land opportunities a few days later. He and her brother Guy traveled by rail and riverboat to Charleston, Missouri, arriving there in February of 1867. Immediately, Joseph began writing letters to Sarah that served as his first fumbling attempts to court her. She shyly responded to his every letter, sometimes as many as one per week, for the course of many months.

Guy Sharits was a veteran of the 7th Tennessee Mounted Infantry and fourteen years Joseph's junior. However, it would seem that he was the more mature of the two travelers. According to Joseph's letters, Guy immediately landed a job while he was simply content to rent a room in a boarding house without putting much effort into finding gainful employment. Perhaps the war had affected Joseph and taken away his ambition, but there were also other things at work.

The U.S. census of 1860, prior to the war, shows Joseph having a four-year-old daughter, Jane. He had no wife, and the census form of that time didn't have an entry to designate marital status. It would seem that he was the widow of an unknown wife, or was abandoned by her. By the 1870 census, daughter Jane too is gone. In his letters to Sarah he hints that the Sharits family is aware of his past and wonders what they would think if they knew he was writing her love letters. Whatever the mystery of his past was, it has been lost to time. His daughter didn't go with him to Missouri, and there is no mention of her in Joseph's correspondence after he came home from the war. Whether she died during his wartime absence or later isn't known, but she disappeared from his life forever. Joseph apparently carried scars that had little to do with his war experiences.

In the multitude of letters sent to Sarah, he boasted of the great fun to be had in Missouri and that he was playing his fiddle at dances and the citizens of the bustling town were paying him well enough for his talent to keep him fed and a roof over his head. Apparently he was an exceptional fiddler, for Sarah repeatedly stated that she missed his playing. Joseph told how he was "getting the greenbacks" playing in Missouri and how he had a "fine chance for fun and a heap of good music." The greenbacks he refers to are Union greenbacks, the paper money issued by the government to replace the gold and silver coinage in use before the Civil War. Joseph also teased Sarah by informing her that there were more pretty girls in Missouri than he had ever suspected. He must have wanted to make her jealous and not outright mad, for he assured her that he and Guy preferred Tennessee girls over even the prettiest of "Missouri tadpoles."

A change becomes evident in Joseph as the letters between him and Sarah progress over the course of months. He began to talk up the business opportunities and available land in Missouri and took a job in a lumberyard paying him fifty dollars a month—healthy wages for a laborer of the day. He complained that he didn't have a horse, and that "a man afoot is nothing." He soon informed Mary that he had gone to a cheaper rooming house to help save his money and was considering buying or renting a home and farm.

Sarah was very educated for a rural young woman of the time, and her handwriting was almost calligraphic. She was shy and modest, and her letters always ended with an apology for her penmanship and grammar. She wrote original song lyrics for Joseph, quoted poetry, and pressed flowers between the pages of her beautiful handwriting. He admitted that he was still fiddling at dances, but that he had nothing to say to any of the girls he saw. In his own words as a former soldier, his heart was "absent without leave" and he longed to see her. He mailed her flower seeds for what is known as a balsam cucumber to cultivate in Tennessee. He gave her careful instructions on how to plant them and care for them, and she continually wrote him updates as to the progress of the tended seeds.

It was not long before Joseph wrote that he had rented a farm and bought a new cook stove for his home. He complained of his lack of culinary skills and the loneliness of the house. She teased him that he and her brother would probably find "Missouri tadpoles to marry" and forget all about Tennessee girls. But it is easy to read between the lines that Joseph had planted seeds of another kind in the rich soil of her heart.

Joseph professed his love and asked her to marry him if he should come for her in September. She was obviously enamored of him, but refused to immediately answer his proposal, citing that "men's minds often wander with the wind from one fancy to another." She protested that she wasn't pretty enough or smart enough to be worth his love. He wrote her, frantically giving her the compliments she was seeking and assuring her that she was the belle of Tennessee.

Her attempts to play hard-to-get did little to hide how she really felt, as seen in the poem she mailed him shortly after his proposal:

> May you be blessed with health and smiles
> While traveling o'er the Western wilds
> And when a lovely home you find,
> Remember the girl you left behind.

Finally, she agreed to marry him, and he promised to come in September to wed her and take her back to Missouri with him. However, throughout his letters he hinted that there were things going on in Charleston that he didn't want to speak of. When she grew impatient with waiting, he finally explained that there was a widespread sickness in the country he had come to. In addition to a strange fever people were falling prey to, there was a cholera outbreak.

Cholera is a bacterial infection of the small intestine that causes severe vomiting and profuse, watery diarrhea. Without city sewage systems, many of the frontier villages and towns contaminated their own drinking water with feces, especially during the rainy season, thus making their citizens susceptible to ingesting the bacteria. Joseph wrote that the weather had been extremely rainy with high waters and flooding along the river, and the conditions were probably perfect for an outbreak. Without intravenous administration of fluids or modern antibiotics, many of those suffering from the disease perished from dehydration. During the 1800s the disease is said to have killed tens of millions of people around the world.

Joseph asked Sarah to wait until September, as he had been reassured by older settlers along the upper Mississippi River that the safest time to travel was during the cold of the coming fall and winter. He explained that most of the people for miles around had been struck ill or dead, while he was healthy as an ox. He feared traveling through miles of disease and begged her to wait until the first hard frost of the winter. He planned to take a wide detour north to avoid a rumored worse disease outbreak east of him. He would take a boat north up the Mississippi, then travel by rail east into Kentucky and south to Knoxville, Tennessee, and from there walk to her home in Morgan County.

On September 16 he wrote that he was starting his trip. His next correspondence was sent eleven days later from Albany, Kentucky, near the Tennessee line. He told her not to worry that he hadn't shown up to claim her and explained that he had been struck down by sickness and was so weak as to be unable to sit up in bed. His convalescence was slow, and he feared he would die among strangers. His last letter, dated October 15, contained a little violet feather among its pages as a token of his esteem. He stated that he was walking weakly and barely able to leave the house he was staying at, but that he would soon be back on his way to her. There are no more letters left to posterity to complete the tale of their romance, but their marriage license is dated November 27, 1867. Joseph had traveled hundreds of miles, some of it on foot, and risked his life to come home to the woman he loved. As a side note, one of her last letters to him before he left Tennessee informed him that the seeds he sent her finally sprouted—love was blooming.

Joseph and Mary lived in Tennessee until sometime after 1870.[78] They had two daughters in the following years, and also took Sarah's sister Mary and her children into their home. It was Mary's husband, John McPhail, who had perished on the *Sultana*.

Both the Sharits and the Spurling families had long been in Tennessee, but Joseph's letters show that he had a touch of wanderlust and was intrigued by the rich soil and seemingly boundless opportunities on the frontier. Something about Minnesota must have struck his fancy, for he and his family show up on a Minnesota territorial and state census in 1875, near his former posting at Leavenworth Station. His bank drafts and checks from 1878 and 1879 were written on a bank in Des Moines, Iowa. It is from there that he migrated to Arkansas.

Somewhere along his travels between Minnesota and Arkansas he had begun to call himself a physician. Billing receipts to his patients show that he was already practicing as a doctor while in Minnesota. It is unknown if he went north to apprentice or to attend medical school. Maybe he simply picked up some basic first aid techniques during the war. His love letters to Sarah in 1867 mentioned that the plant seeds he sent her had medicinal value, and he seemed to have some knowledge of or at least an interest in medicine even back then.

As an interesting side note, William Worrall Mayo, founder of the famous Mayo Clinic, led a party of volunteers from St. Paul and Le Sueur to the prairies of western Minnesota during the Sioux outbreak of late 1862 and 1863. They treated soldiers' injuries and attended to the plight of the many refugees who had been burned out by rampaging Indians or were simply too scared to remain at their farms. Madelia, one of Joseph's posts during his time as a Galvanized Yankee, was right in the path of the fleeing settlers. Mayo was also a military medical examiner for the Rochester, Minnesota, draft board during the last two years of the Civil War. His home in that city wasn't far to the east of Leavenworth, another of Joseph's former postings and the settlement he came back to in the 1870s. It is not inconceivable that the two crossed paths, or perhaps the volunteer and military doctors of the Sioux scare inspired Joseph to become a physician.

No matter how Joseph came to be a doctor, licensing and training for medical practitioners of the time was not standardized as it is now. In many states and the frontier territories a man who wished to be a physician could simply hang out his shingle and advertise himself as such, medical school diploma or not. Rural people couldn't be picky about who they could get to tend their ailments. Two of his neighbors in Benton County, Arkansas, were doctors themselves, and there are many receipts among his doctor's kit attesting to the fact that he had a lively medical practice before going to live near his sister in Montgomery County.[79]

The doctor of old was not only a physician, but most often a pharmacist as well. The traveling bag that hung from his saddle horn or sat upon his buggy seat was his mobile apothecary. Among Joseph's medical kit are measuring scales to mix various compounds, along with a mortar and pestle. Tiny square glass bottles are labeled with strange element names, and prescriptions and drug recipes written upon note cards sound more like the wish list of a mad scientist or an alchemist than a doctor.

Two items from Joseph's trunk, passed down through the family, shed light on the extent of his medical knowledge, as well as the limited science and odd practices of the time. Joseph owned two medical journals. One was a thick tome titled *Gunn's New Family Physician*.[80] Within its 1,200 pages of technical writing and illustrated drawings it is easy to see the beginnings of modern medicine and the acceptance of Louis Pasteur's germ theory, albeit the field of human medicine obviously had a long way to go. Many of the treatments and prescriptions for various diseases in Gunn's journal sound more like the cures of a village witch doctor. Crushed cranberries are claimed to cure skin cancer and tumors, and a report from the Academy of Medicine in Paris states that French researchers supposedly observed small animals like lice residing within cancerous sores. Scholars and theorists forming the cutting edge of medicine at the time recommended brandy, double chloride of mercury, arsenic, or silver nitrate to kill those parasites and to cure most types of cancer.

The second book upon which Joseph based his studies was *Home Remedies for Man and Beast*.[81] Along with cures for common ailments, the book includes instructions for everything from doctoring livestock to etiquette. It would seem the difference between a doctor and a country veterinarian wasn't very great—as long as both had fine manners. Young gentlemen are advised to take off their hats in a lady's presence when indoors, and to simply tip the brim of their headgear when outdoors. Diagrams for the proper folding of table napkins and suggestions on polite dinner conversation are found not far from the cure for a faulty bladder and hemorrhoids. Apparently, nineteenth-century readers found it not at all odd for instructions on how to shoe a mean horse to be in the same book with remedies for menstruating women with cramps and sore breasts. Upon reading the little book, Joseph should have been able to tell a horse's age by its teeth, treat whooping cough, cure a sick pig, deliver a baby, properly adjust a woman's corset, or identify cholera bacteria under a microscope. What a wonderful age when the arriving gentleman doctor could tend to your pneumonia and treat your milk cow's hoof rot in the same house call.

Some of the remedies for disease are quaint, if not downright scary, and will leave the modern reader appreciating the advances of modern medicine. Victims bitten by a rabid dog are advised to immediately "suck the wound thoroughly" to avoid getting hydrophobia. A little turpentine, tobacco, rhubarb, and castor oil is said to be a sure cure for wormy children. Rags soaked in kerosene or carbolic acid will do double duty to treat a laceration or to get rid of ticks, chiggers, and other external parasites. According to the author, male pattern baldness can be cured and hair regrown by mixing whiskey, glycerin, quinine, and water in a bowl and rubbing the concoction on the scalp every day. Constipation is seen as the vilest cause of disease and poor health. Slippery elm bark, molasses, castor oil, and other various remedies supposedly ensure a healthy bowel movement and thus, a long and vigorous life.

In defense of the book, there are parts that show some scientific accuracy. Personal hygiene is listed as a priority of good health, and bathing and cleanliness of wounds are sworn by. The public is urged to take at least one bath a week (whether it's needed or not). Also, cleanly citizens are advised to thoroughly wash and comb their hair with soap and water at least every two weeks for healthy and luxurious locks. Given that there were no stick deodorants in the nineteenth century, a world filled with once-a-week bathers was probably highly odiferous, to say the least. The author seems to have that in mind when he provides the recipe for perfumes among his pages. Modern medicine may not be perfect, but medical knowledge has certainly come a long way.

While the extent of Joseph's medical skills aren't known, he did perhaps possess some King Solomon–type wisdom. A family story tells of one of his house calls and a unique treatment. He arrived at the home of a lady who had many mysterious ailments. She was supposedly so weak as to be unable to walk more than a few steps and apparently had done very little for the previous year other than to lie in her bed or sit in her rocking chair. Her family was cooking and cleaning for her and called Joseph in to find out what was wrong with her. Her long list of symptoms seemed to fit no known illness. She had no fever or physical signs of injury or disease, and possessed a perfectly healthy appetite. He finally instructed the woman's family to put a large dose of salt in her food and for them not to keep drinking water in the house. When asked by the family about his strange prescription he laughed. He said the salt would make her thirsty, and she would have to get her lazy self out of the house to have a drink. Apparently he was right, for the hypochondriac was miraculously able to walk to the water well. Her family observed the healthy and leisurely manner in which she strolled across the yard and immediately declared her miraculously cured and fit and ready to do her own chores.

When Joseph showed up in Montgomery County with his wife in the late 1880s he had a shiny black buggy and a driver to chauffeur him to house calls.[82] In his mid-fifties, five feet nine, with a long, pale beard and black suit, he cut quite a swath among the locals. But what may have most impressed the mountain folks, at least the young bachelors, were the pretty young daughters he brought with him. One of those fair maidens caught Franklin Cogburn's eye.

Anna Belle Spurling was eighteen in 1888, and different than the mountain gals Franklin had grown up around and danced with at various social events. She was slim and willowy with a quick smile, blue eyes, and blond hair as yellow as an ear of Montgomery County sweet corn. Annie, as she was known, would in later years refer to herself as a "Tennessee lady."[83] Like her mother, she was a devout Christian and always made it to church on the Sabbath. She was bright and educated and could play a piano when one was available. School honor roll cards dating from 1880 attest to her wits. Franklin had very little schooling and couldn't read nor write. Like many of the boys of the county born in the wake of the war, he had grown up barefoot and ignorant of anything but the woodlands and the hard work it took to make a mountain farm produce. If Annie was a polished gem, Franklin was the veritable chunk of coal. Nevertheless, that didn't prevent him from falling in love with her, or her with him.

It is uncertain how long he had known her or courted her before she finally agreed to marry him. Annie often told her children and grandchildren that she had seen Franklin's face on the water while looking down into the well long before she ever met him. An old mountain folk belief was that a girl could sometimes see her future husband's reflection if she looked into a well. Fate seemed to have brought them together, and without a doubt their love was strong. Better than a century later, I discovered a braided lock of her hair in a little glass case tucked in Franklin's leather billfold.

On September 13, 1888, they tied the knot at the same time the Fort Smith court was preparing official writs of arrest for Franklin and Fayette. Joseph Spurling sat on the porch and surveyed the occasion with his rifle across his lap, stroking his long beard thoughtfully. For better or worse, the boy was now his son-in-law, but at least Franklin had sand. Perhaps the young lovers brought back memories of Joseph's youth courting Annie's mother, and maybe he broke out his fiddle and played a tune or two for old time's sake.

Carter Markham, Franklin's stepfather, hangman's rope scars and all, performed the marriage rites. Armed members of the clan served as witnesses while others stood watch over the trails in and out of Fancy Hill. If it was anything like many a holiday and mountain wedding, it is safe to assume that the lookouts got a turn dancing to whatever tune the fiddle player could manage and a tug at a jug full of mountain dew. Annie may have frowned at her wedding guests partaking of spirits, but it would seem, then as now, that some women are just drawn to bad boys.

8

Murderers Row

During what might be considered Franklin and Annie's honeymoon, the Law was working feverishly to plan the breakup of the Cogburn moonshiners and bring Trammell's murderers to justice. A writ of arrest had been issued for Fayette Cogburn for his indictment by a grand jury on whiskey charges. However, that writ was never executed. In September, another writ was issued for his arrest for the murder of J. D. Trammell. The deputy marshals again had no luck arresting Fayette, perhaps because they had stopped trying. As they had found out earlier, riding through the brush to locate Cogburns could be a little unhealthy. Their big hats and badges made too pretty a target for any would-be marksman. Despite many in that portion of the county turning against Trammell's murderers, nobody was willing to lend a hand when it came to catching the outlaws. And there were still plenty of Cogburns to keep an eye out and aid each other.

There is an old family tale that Franklin Cogburn saw a deputy marshal riding up the trail in the vicinity of his home. The deputy marshals, in general, had been of great annoyance and trouble to the family. Franklin rested his rifle on a tree limb and watched the lawman ride by the foot of the ridge below him, unaware that he was under the gun, so to speak. Franklin cocked his Winchester and took a fine bead on the deputy. It would have been an easy shot, but he didn't pull the trigger. Killing a man from ambush wasn't his style. He had no problem shooting at Parker's boys in defense of his life or family, but he wasn't low-down enough to shoot a man in the back. There might have been more Cogburns waiting down the road who weren't nearly as scrupulous and discriminating when it came to rifle targets.

It is also said that Franklin issued a challenge to Deputy Marshal Reuben Fry. It was Fry who had signed the original affidavit that got the Cogburns indicted for moonshining. It was also Fry's testimony that identified Franklin as Trammell's murderer. Franklin let it be known through word of mouth that if Fry wanted to come back down to Montgomery County, he was more than welcome.

There was a certain large tree along the trail from Fancy Hill to Black Springs with some peculiar characteristics that made it easily identifiable. Perhaps it was lightning struck or unusually large, or had a twisted trunk or strangely shaped limbs that made it a landmark. Supposedly, during the time the deputy marshals were prowling around questioning folks and trying to corner Franklin and Fayette, a suspicious Mexican claiming to be a horse trader showed up in the area. He told folks that he had ridden up from Hickory Station because he had heard there were some good horses that could be bought in the area. He was well mounted and well armed and spent more time asking questions about the Cogburns than he did talking about horses. He was also very curious about the lay of the land around Fancy Hill and everything south of Black Springs. It was thought that he might be after the reward offered for the capture of Trammell's killers. The Mexican disappeared as quickly as he had arrived without ever letting his intentions be known, but a few locals whispered afterward that he had been killed and buried in a rocky draw near the tree. That landmark became known as the Mexican Tree.

If Reuben Fry desired, Franklin would gladly have met him at the Mexican Tree anytime to shoot it out. The two could settle their differences once and for all, like knights of old in a trial by combat to prove who was in the right. It didn't matter if that field of combat was in the piney woods of Arkansas with nobody to witness but the birds and the bees instead of some palace court with pennants flying above the fair damsels and ladies-in-waiting. Obviously this never happened, for neither man died of bullet wounds that year.

Most of the deputy marshals out of Fort Smith weren't so stupid as to risk fights when they didn't have to. They were paid to bring in criminals and fugitives, not for giving their enemies fair shakes in gun duels. Only *Gunsmoke*'s Marshal Matt Dillon walked out into the streets of Dodge City, Hollywood, and gave his foes a chance at slapping leather with him. But then again, he had a free beer tab at the Longhorn Saloon. If Reuben Fry had shown up at the Mexican Tree, he'd have had a straight-shooting posse with him and a stout pair of handcuffs to fit Franklin's wrists.

The Cogburns' extensive moonshine business had made them connections for a far piece around them. Many of their cronies advised Franklin and Fayette to hide out in the Nations for a time until things cooled off and the Law forgot about them. No badge packer was going to arrest anyone who didn't want to be found over in the Winding Stair, Kiamichi, and Sans Bois mountains a day's long ride to the west. Many of the locales in what is now Oklahoma still bear the names of outlaw hideouts—Robbers Cave, Horse Thief Springs, Younger's Bend, Marlow Outlaw Cave, and more.

Even Annie was willing to move to the Nations, or anywhere, for that matter, if her new husband was bound and determined to avoid arrest. But Franklin wasn't having any part of running. A new start somewhere that the Law wasn't looking for him sounded good, but his roots, family, and everything else he knew were right there in Montgomery County. Annie didn't deserve to be dragged around the country as a fugitive, and the two of them had a baby on the way. He had rented some farmland and intended to plant more acreage come spring. He was going to keep a close watch out for the Law and stay right where he was.

Many in the family were beginning to think that defending themselves in court might be preferable to shooting it out with the Law. The Hanging Judge wasn't ever going to run out of deputies to send their way, and many a man who had committed worse crimes had hired a fancy lawyer and walked out of that court scot-free.

At the same time, the U.S. Marshal and prosecutors were planning a new tactic. By 1889, it was plain that the Cogburns had personal grudges against many of the deputies who had thus far worked the case, many of them Confederate veterans who were believed to bear prejudice against Mountain Federals. What the court needed were local men to pin badges on. W. J. "Jack" Hopper, the postmaster and storekeeper who had helped them get Bill Cogburn out of Black Springs half a year earlier, was signed on as a Deputy U.S. Marshal. Hopper was friends with many of the Cogburns and had been a Mountain Federal himself. Later in the year, E. R. Box, who lived near Caddy Gap, took the oath of office. Box was a Confederate veteran, but had no bad history with the Cogburns.

Jack Hopper understood the Cogburns. He had originally joined with the Confederacy near the beginning of the war, but swapped sides and signed up with the 1st Arkansas Infantry. He and Fayette Cogburn had become friends during their service together. Hopper was at odds with many of his Tennessee

John Franklin "Rooster" Cogburn sepia portrait.

William Isaac "Bill" Cogburn (left) and John Franklin "Rooster" Cogburn (right), circa 1884. *(Courtesy of Jim Sanders)*

Deputy U.S. Marshal John David Trammell and his first wife, Clara Andrews.
(Courtesy of Matthew Barry Hart)

J. D. Trammell. *(Courtesy of Matthew Barry Hart)*

James Lafayette Cogburn in his later years. *(Courtesy of Dorothy Mims)*

Old Montgomery County Courthouse, circa 1885.
(Courtesy of the Heritage House Museum of Montgomery County)

Old Montgomery County Courthouse, circa 1890.
(Courtesy of Shirley Shewmake Manning)

Brigadier General Stand
Watie. *(Courtesy of the
Oklahoma Historical Society)*

Judge Isaac C. Parker.
*(Courtesy of the Oklahoma
Historical Society)*

Deputy U.S. Marshal Dave Rusk posed with other deputy marshals and posse members after killing the Cherokee outlaw Ned Christie. Dave is the little guy seated in the front row, far left.

(Courtesy of the Oklahoma Historical Society)

Deputy U.S. Marshal W. J. "Jack" Hopper. *(Courtesy of James Chaffin)*

The Prince of Hangmen, George Maledon. *(Courtesy of the Fort Smith Museum of History)*

Bill Cogburn's .41 Colt Thunderer. *(Courtesy of Jim Sanders)*

Garrison Avenue in Fort Smith in the 1880s.
(Courtesy of the Fort Smith Museum of History)

Another view of Garrison Avenue in Fort Smith in the 1880s.
(Courtesy of the Fort Smith Museum of History)

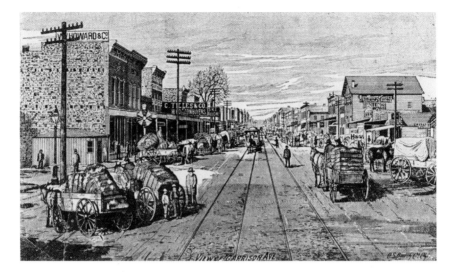

Lithograph of Garrison Avenue in Fort Smith, 1887.
(Courtesy of the Fort Smith Museum of History)

Pioneers either heading out from Fort Smith or arriving there.
(Courtesy of the Fort Smith Museum of History)

Cherokee Bill's hanging in 1896. This is the only known photo of one of Judge Parker's executions (photos weren't allowed). *(Courtesy of the Fort Smith Museum of History)*

Deputy U.S. Marshal Cal Whitson standing on the porch of his grocery store. *(Courtesy of* True West *magazine)*

Three of J. D. Trammell's daughters posed in front of his home northeast of Huntington, Arkansas, in the 1920s.
(Courtesy of Matthew Barry Hart)

Joseph Spurling (Annie Cogburn's father and Franklin "Rooster" Cogburn's father-in-law).

Joseph Spurling's second wife, Sarah Malvina Sharits (Annie Cogburn's mother).

Anna Belle Cogburn in her later years with daughter Laura Belle Cook and grandchildren.

Burris sawmill/gristmill, Montgomery County, circa 1888.

J. D. Trammell and his second wife, Mary Willie Neal.

(Courtesy of Matthew Barry Hart)

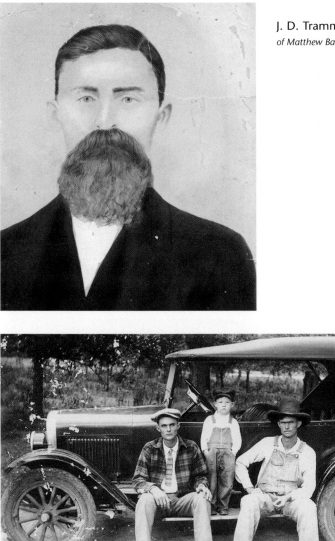

J. D. Trammell. *(Courtesy of Matthew Barry Hart)*

Left to right: Claude Cogburn, Thomas Cogburn, Guy Cogburn, 1920s.

Claude Cogburn
holding daughter Ruby
on a prized colt.

Joseph Spurling's Model 1892 Winchester, .32-20 caliber.

Fort Smith Courthouse and U.S. jail.
(Courtesy of the Fort Smith Museum of History)

family members over his decision to side with the Union, but he found like minds among the Mountain Federals like the Cogburns. His store, at what would become the community of Hopper, Arkansas, was the nearest such enterprise to Fancy Hill, and he had more firsthand information about the events of Trammell's demise than any of those officials at Fort Smith.

Relying on Jack Hopper, a writ of arrest for Franklin Cogburn was issued on January 28, 1889. On February 26, Hopper showed up at Franklin's home. Franklin watched him come up the road, and several other family members spread out in the yard with their guns at hand. Hopper didn't come unarmed, but he did come alone. Every Cogburn there knew he had pinned on a badge, but he ignored their hot stares and rode up in the middle of them. He stopped his horse at the edge of the porch where Franklin and Annie stood waiting.

He calmly explained to Franklin that there was no avoiding the Law unless he fled the country. It was only a matter of time before he was arrested or worse. What Hopper said made sense, and every person there admired his honesty and the courage he displayed riding in there alone. Franklin's brother Bill had shown up to face liquor charges in the Montgomery County circuit court and received only a $200 fine just days before.[84] There was a chance that Franklin could find leniency in Parker's court, or even prove his innocence. The way Hopper put it, there was no sense in fighting the inevitable and risking harm to his family in the process. He claimed that there never was going to be peace and quiet in Montgomery County until Franklin's crime was settled.

Hopper was invited to take dinner with the family, and sometime later in the day, Franklin agreed to surrender if he was given some time to get his affairs in order.[85] The brave deputy marshal agreed, and in early March, Franklin rode up to the store at Hopper and turned himself in. A few days later, March 7, Hopper lodged Franklin in the US. jail at Fort Smith.[86]

Of the other men wanted for questioning or prosecution in Trammell's death, Deputy Hopper had little luck bringing them in. Fayette Cogburn discussed the matter with him, but was unwilling to turn himself in. Maybe he was going to wait and see how Franklin fared in the Hanging Judge's court before he committed to anything.

Deputy Marshals Reuben Fry and Otis Wheeler always had trouble trying to pin down exactly who the five men were who had approached Trammell at the crossroads. John Barnett was questioned and no murder charges were brought against him, even though the grand jury had indicted him. He either wasn't believed to be the shooter or hadn't even been present when Trammell was killed. Despite his exoneration for the death of Trammell, a writ for his arrest was issued for illegal distilling and retail liquor sales without a license. The law never brought him to the court for a trial, and the writs were allowed to go out of date. It is unknown if he fled the county for a while or simply hid out closer to home.

As mentioned earlier, Nathan Owensby fled to the Nations or to other parts unknown. Some of Montgomery County's moonshiners were going elsewhere or quitting the trade—just what the Fort Smith court wanted.

Charlie Johnson, the last of the five wanted men, disappeared for a long time. It is unclear just who he was. Charlie was supposedly a young man during the time Trammell was killed, and there was a teenage Charles Johnson in neighboring Polk County in 1880. Parker's court listed an alias for the Charles Johnson they wanted: Walter Piles. U.S. census records of 1870 do show a Walter Piles in Sebastian County, Arkansas, of which Fort Smith was the county seat. A man named Walter Piles was charged with moonshining in Yell County in 1886 during Deputy Marshal Trammell's first attempts at arresting moonshiners for Judge Parker, but was never brought to justice. It is possible that there was bad blood between Trammell and Piles before the lawman ever came to Montgomery County. None of Franklin's fellow moonshiners are alive to identify their friend's true name, and it is impossible to glean his identity from the spotty court records. There are some clues that suggest he was somehow kin to Henry Cogburn's wife, whose maiden name was Johnson. Rumors had him hiding out in Texas. Charlie Johnson, alias Walter Piles, remains a mystery.

Charlie Johnson was ruled in contempt of court over his failure to appear on liquor charges in 1889. For many years, descendants of Franklin Cogburn claimed that Franklin had never shot a deputy marshal, but had simply been found in contempt of court during legal proceedings. Memories can be fickle things, and Charlie's story may have been mixed up with Franklin's.

His friends may have hidden out, but Franklin was not alone at Fort Smith. He had over 125 other prisoners crammed into the jail alongside the courthouse to keep him company.[87] Perhaps he should have thanked his lucky stars he wasn't confined back before 1877, when men were locked in one of two dark, moldy, rock-floored basement rooms underneath the courthouse. A man might welcome the gallows after months in that dungeon, eating vermin-infested food and wallowing in filth.

As it was, Franklin was housed in a cell on the lower floor of the new jail at the southwest end of the old barracks that served as the Hanging Judge's courthouse. The new federal lockup was built with a three-story steel, brick, and stucco cage standing inside it. There was a seven-feet space between the cage and the walls of the building on three sides, and stairways on the ends adjoining the courtroom. An iron-grated catwalk marked the perimeter of the second and third levels. The first floor was reserved for those charged with murder and was affectionately known as "Murderers Row."[88] The other two floors were for criminals of a supposedly less violent nature—burglars, robbers, and bruisers on the second, and whiskey-makers and peddlers on the third. A hallway down the center divided each floor into two rows of twelve outward-facing cells, numbered odd on one side and even on the other.[89]

The five-by-seven-feet cells all had a steel-lattice door and a levered locking system to secure them. There were no windows in the stucco walls, and the only light that penetrated the cells came slanting through the door or spilled into a small metal hatch at the rear of the room when a prisoner's chamber pot was being emptied. Besides the slop bucket, the only other furnishing of those dark, tiny closets were blankets and two steel cots stacked into bunk beds. Although the prison plans called for two prisoners per cell, three and four were sometimes forced to share the tight space. Despite the guards' careful watch, a steady supply of contraband was smuggled inside the jail. Already deadly men stashed a variety of knives, shanks, and other cutting weapons to use at their leisure on whoever struck their fancy. Occasionally prisoners were able to equip themselves with a pistol for an escape attempt. During the day, the cell doors were opened to let the prisoners walk around, but only on the level that housed them. Rough banter echoed within the masonry walls of the jail when the guards brought in or took out a prisoner.

On quiet days, the prisoners could hear the thump of the sandbag dummies being dropped from the gallows outside as the executioner, George Maledon, stretched his ropes and tested his trapdoors in preparation for another hanging. Maledon, in a September 25, 1887, *Chicago Daily Tribune* interview, lists the meticulous attention he gave to his craft:

> I always prepare the ropes a week or more before the day of execution and stretch them with dummies, adjusting the trap and letting them fall through five or six times each day. The condemned men al-

ways know when I am preparing for them, as they can easily hear the noise made by dummies falling through. They frequently ask me how she works, etc., sometimes in a sincere and sometimes in a jocular manner. While only fifty-two have been hung I have prepared ropes for nearly a hundred, many death sentences having been commuted to life imprisonment after their ropes had been prepared."

[Reporter] They all know you, and are aware of your duties, I suppose, long before their day of execution arrives?

O, yes, my duties as guard at the jail throw me in contact with them every day for months. Frequently they ask me on the gallows to make a sure job, and I always tell them to follow my instructions and there will be no mistake. The main thing for them to do is not to move their heads after the rope is adjusted, and in nearly every case they do just as I tell them. I always shake the hand of each one and bid them good-by just before pulling the black caps over, and I have become so accustomed to it that it is no more than bidding farewell to a friend who is starting out on a journey, perhaps never to return.

It might have been that Maledon was preparing for the hanging of James Mills and Malachi Allen scheduled for April 19, 1889. Mills and a friend, both African Americans, had killed a man in the Seminole Nation, Indian Territory. They had shot him in the back and then twice in the mouth as he lay dying. A mob tried to arrest them and a fight ensued. Mills's partner died later of his wounds, but Mills escaped only to be caught later. Malachi Allen, another African American outlaw, murdered a man in an argument over a saddle out in the Chickasaw Nation. He then shot it out with Deputy Marshal McAlester and his posse. The lawmen winged him badly enough that his arm had to be amputated after he was brought to Fort Smith for trial. Judge Parker gave one-armed criminals no special mercy, and Allen was to hang by his neck until he was dead, dead, dead.

George Maledon, hangman and jailer, was a Bavarian by birth. The oft published picture of him with his long beard and two butt-forward pistols on his hips has come to epitomize the Hanging Judge's brand of justice. Although portrayed in his day and since as something akin to the Grim Reaper and known as the Prince of Hangmen, the former Detroit machinist and Union artilleryman considered himself a professional working a necessary job. He thought the men he hung deserved what they got, but derived no pleasure from their executions.[90] However, he did state that there were "many who deserved it more than others."[91]

While Maledon wasn't a big man and was kind to those he had to hang, he was no pushover when it came to his other duties as a guard at the federal jail. While a Sebastian County deputy sheriff or a jailer, he shot three horse thieves who were attempting to escape, killing one.[92] Maledon was supposedly an excellent pistol shot. As the turnkey at the U.S. Jail at Fort Smith, he dropped Frank Butler with one shot at a supposed distance of seventy-five yards as that prisoner was escaping. Ellis McGhee, who was also making a bid for freedom, was also shot, but survived.[93] He is also famous for his answer when questioned by a lady if he was bothered by his victims' ghosts. He reportedly replied, "No, I have never hanged a man who came back to have the job done over."[94] There is another version where Deputy U.S. Marshal Heck Thomas asked him the

very same question. Maledon supposedly told him that he figured he had hung the ghosts too.

The scaffold Maledon practiced his deadly art upon had a
trap thirty inches wide by twenty feet long, and twelve men
could stand side by side under the stout overhead wooden
beam to be hung at the same time.[95] He gave all the condemned—white men, red men, and black men—equal treatment in the form of the same six-foot drop with a carefully
oiled and stretched hemp rope knotted neatly around their
necks. Some of the doomed broke down and cried while walking to the gallows, while other men were calm and cool. Some
got religion and confessed their sins, and others glared at the
crowd or mocked the whole proceedings. Aaron Wilson, a vicious murderer who scalped his victims, had a Catholic priest
hold an umbrella over his head to shade him while he stood on
the gallows and smoked a last cigar and listened to the U.S.
Marshal read his death warrant. William Brown fainted on the
way to the gallows. Colorado Bill Elliott kept his sense of
humor, and when Maledon was putting the rope over his neck
remarked, "For God's sake, boys, break our necks and don't
punish us."[96]

As Franklin passed the slow hours in jail, he must have wondered how he would handle himself if a jury found him guilty
of Trammell's murder. The Hanging Judge was a notorious
stickler for the letter of the law when it came to sentencing.
Murder called for capital punishment, and every man in the jail
knew that was just what a convicted killer would get if some
last-minute pardon or Supreme Court ruling didn't save his
neck. Franklin's life hung in the balance of the scales of justice.

While in jail, Franklin was surrounded by some of the worst
cutthroats and villains the States and the Indian Nations had to
offer, and even a dog. On March 25, 1888, Jack Spaniard was
locked in a cell on Murderers Row. He and an accomplice,

Frank Palmer, were accused of ambushing and killing Deputy U.S. Marshal William Irwin in 1886 near Pheasant Bluff on the Arkansas River, the same location where Stand Watie had captured the *J. R. Williams* years before. A $500 reward was placed on the outlaws' heads. The accomplice got away, but Spaniard was captured. In a most unusual presentation of evidence, Spaniard's dog was brought in and kept at the U.S. jail for months awaiting trial. The dog had been seen with Spaniard and Palmer prior to Irwin's murder from ambush and wasn't seen with them when they went down the road afterward. The dog wasn't with them because it had remained behind and was found with Irwin's body. During Spaniard's trial, he denied the dog was his. His pet was brought into the courtroom, and the loyal mutt immediately went to his master when released, leaving the jury no doubt as to who he belonged to. It is probably the only time in recorded history where a dog was called to witness in a murder trial. His testimony got Spaniard convicted and hung.

Fortunately, Franklin wasn't long in jail with the dog or any of the other mongrels locked up there. He was brought before Judge Parker in early April. His official court date was set for August 7 due to a large backlog of cases.[97] The family chipped in money to help Franklin's cause, and somehow he was released until his trial date. Maybe his turning himself in had some sway with the judge and prosecutor, or the lawyer he hired did his job and bond was set and paid. Whatever the case, Franklin was a free man, if only for a little while. He could still run.

9

United States vs. Franklin Cogburn

Franklin didn't run. He was going to take his chances before the Hanging Judge later in the year. Deputies Jack Hopper and E. R. Box showed up twice during the summer to serve many of the Cogburn clan with subpoenas to appear as witnesses in Franklin's trial, fifteen of them in all.[98] Many people recommended that Franklin hire the services of the famous defense lawyer J. Warren Reed. Although recently come to Fort Smith, Reed had already defended many criminals there in widely publicized trials. In the years to come he would get many a jury to return a verdict of innocent or manage to arrange pardons and appeals to the U.S. Supreme Court.

Despite Reed's notoriety and skills, his fees were beyond what Franklin could afford. During Reed's tenure as a defense lawyer in the Fort Smith court, there were those who said hiring him was like making a deal with the Devil. His price was at least as high as old Lucifer's, and he would leave you without a pair of pants to your name and take the skin off your back when he could. There were wild rumors, many of them spread by outlaws, that he often took the defendant's family land in hock for his services. Some even claimed that he had worked for treasure maps leading to stashed stolen loot or promises of a cut of his defendants' future robberies. The moonshining had slowed to a crawl with so much of the court's attention on Montgomery County, and money was in short supply among all the Cogburns. Franklin wasn't about to indebt or starve his family by hiring Reed.

Franklin kept the services of the lawyer, name unknown, who had attended his hearing the previous spring. The fellow may not have been as competent as Reed, but he didn't require the Cogburns to hock the farm either. In fact, legend has it that the man wasn't too bad a sort, as far as lawyers go. Whoever he was, if his courtroom antics were anything like his eccentric behavior, then he certainly could put on a good show for a jury.

The story goes that Franklin's lawyer had nothing against a man making moonshine and, in fact, imbibed of all kinds of whiskey quite freely. He was a portly man who refused to wear a hat because he had once been forced to fight a duel over forgetting to tip his headgear to a wealthy sugarcane planter's sister when passing her in town. When he walked along the streets of Fort Smith he carried a woman's fancy parasol propped on his shoulder to shelter his bald head from the sun.

He kept a one-eyed crippled bulldog chained to his desk that would growl every time his master would ring the office's brass spittoon with a stream of plug tobacco or screech his chair legs on the wooden floor. The dog wouldn't let anyone step over him or pass too close to his chosen spot on the floor without raising his hackles and showing the slobbery, worn-out nubs of his fangs. When asked why he tolerated the mutt growling at his customers, the lawyer always said that he owed it to the dog to take care of him, no matter how ill-tempered and neurotic he became in his old age. Apparently, the bulldog had once saved his life by biting him. The resulting wound prevented the lawyer from getting on a train that eventually crashed and killed many passengers of the coach he was to be riding.

In June of 1889, Page Cogburn was tried and found guilty of selling moonshine without a license. Two days later a jury returned a verdict of not guilty on a second charge of illegal distilling. The *Fort Smith Elevator* states that Page received a year in jail as a result of the first trial, but the court documents do not show that he was sent to a federal prison. They do show that he was handed over to the U.S. jail at Fort Smith. By this time, many whiskey offenders were serving their time in that jail, and that may have been the case for Page. Regardless, the bull of the woods of the Cogburn moonshiners had his horns tipped. In an attempt to stomp hard on the Cogburns' operation, Page was also fined $1,000, supposedly to offset the taxes and licensing fees he had avoided since his original indictment in 1886 for moonshining. When he couldn't pay the fine, a lien was levied against his property for indebtedness. It was beginning to look like the Law had the upper hand.

By August 7, the day of Franklin's trial, Annie was seven months pregnant with their first child. She, her father, and many of the Cogburns and allies traveled north with Franklin. The Fort Smith of 1889 was a bustling Victorian city with a steady supply of goods and travelers arriving via the steamboats plying the Arkansas River or the railroad. Its citizens bragged it was the most modern, fanciest city south and west of Chicago. The wooden boardwalks of its frontier beginnings were already being replaced by concrete sidewalks. Mule-drawn trolleys worked those concourses of the city, and gas lampposts lit the way at night. There was a telephone exchange, and electricity was just a few years around the bend.

Normally, a trip to the town to see the electric lights, streetcars, and other sights was somewhat akin to a vacation for country folks, but not on that day. In the early morning hours, Franklin and his family passed somberly down Garrison Av-

98 / *Brett Cogburn*

enue under the shadow of the tall, narrow-windowed brick buildings. Citizens going about their business or walking to the courthouse for the day's proceedings gawked openly at the Cogburns. Watching worried families coming and going from Parker's courtroom was an everyday occurrence for people who lived and worked in that part of the city. Those who stared at Franklin and his family couldn't be blamed for speculating as to what crimes had brought them there.

If it seemed there were more people in town than usual, it was perhaps because of the hanging of Jack Spaniard and William Walker to take place at noon of that day.[99] A fair with days of horse racing was also being held during the week. There was nothing like a hanging and a fair to stir up business along the avenue. But there had been a day when there would have been far more people in town.

Supposedly, five thousand men, women, and children had shown up to watch the first sextet Parker had ever hung side by side in 1875. Even more spectators were present when Maledon dropped the trap on five more in 1876. With the newspapers touting the novelty of multiple public executions across the United States, it is no wonder that the horrid affairs drew such immense crowds. And the onlookers weren't just locals. Fans of such morbid entertainment traveled by horse and train and shank's mare from miles away and outlying states to view the ghastly proceedings. During the early years of Parker's court, there was at the hangings a festive atmosphere akin to a Sunday picnic, barbecue, or a modern-day sports event. Those who could not procure a room for the night or afford it pitched lean-tos and tents outside of town or slept in their wagons. Whiskey peddlers worked the perimeters of the masses outside the courthouse grounds selling refreshments to those so inclined. In some ways it was like fans tailgating prior to an NFL football game.

At the appointed time the condemned men were paraded to

the scaffold. Local clergymen led the crowd in singing hymns, often joined by the prisoners, and then the U.S. Marshal read aloud the death warrants and the crimes the men were to die for. Once this was done, each prisoner was allowed a final statement to the crowd before Maledon slipped black hoods and hangman's nooses over their heads.

And if watching a man drop six feet to come to a sudden halt at the end of a rope was not enough, the crowd was often treated to an even more gruesome sight. Despite Maledon's pride in his skill as a hangman, and his later claims to the contrary, not every man died a quick and painless death from a broken neck. Of the five men hung simultaneously in 1876, only one of them was dead after the drop. The jerking, twitching bodies dangled pitifully under the scaffold, and one of the outlaws was heard to moan and gasp as he strangled to death. It was almost ten minutes before all five were dead. In 1882, it took Ed Fulsom an hour to strangle to death, and John Thornton nearly had his head ripped off his shoulders in 1892.[100]

Other parts of the country had long since gone to private executions, and the public hangings at Fort Smith appalled many in Washington D.C. No matter if such grisly executions could serve to show the masses the wages of sin, the purpose of the courts was to uphold and maintain civilization, not to relish barbarism like the criminals it sentenced. Under pressure from the Justice Department, a high-fenced enclosure was built around the gallows in 1878. Only a small group of fifty or so was allowed inside to serve as witnesses to hangings from that time on. The huge crowds and Roman circus that had once gone hand in hand with the Fort Smith executions were to be no more. Some local shopkeepers and businessmen claimed that the new policy hurt city revenue, but it is said that progress has its price.

Like his hangings, Parker's daily court proceedings drew numbers of interested observers. However, in contrast to the unruly gathering that once took place when criminals were getting their necks stretched, his courtroom was quiet and orderly despite the public in the galleries. Bailiffs and deputy marshals were at the courthouse doors to see that nobody brought firearms into the proceedings. Those who laughed once too often or too loudly at some witty defense attorney's remarks might find themselves escorted from the room.

A defendant looking out the courtroom's tall, narrow windows couldn't help but notice the roof of the hanging gallows on the lawn. It must have been a hard thought for Annie that her husband stood a chance of having to one day stand on that execution platform. Franklin probably didn't care much for the view either.

Franklin's proceedings were the first of the morning. He sat beside his lawyer facing the Hanging Judge at his bench. The past years hadn't been kind to the judge, and his goatee had long since begun to fade to white and his portly body was beginning to give over to fat and a potbelly that threatened the buttons of his vest. The two men took each other's measure, the space of only a few feet between them—the man who sought to bring justice to the Western District of Arkansas, and the outlaw. The judge's stare from under his shaggy brows must have been a match for the flinty gleam of Franklin's dark, defiant eyes.

Franklin's trial took the better part of three days. One by one, witnesses in the Trammell murder case were called by the prosecution and defense. Many of the witnesses for the defense swore to Franklin's good name. They claimed that Deputy Trammell had brought his fate upon himself by his strong-arm tactics, but that it wasn't Franklin who pulled the trigger. But none of them were present at the crossroads when Trammell was killed. The defense lawyer tried to draw upon the jury's sentiment by pointing out that Franklin was a newlywed and soon to be a father.

The prosecution portrayed the Cogburns as a ruthless gang of moonshiners, just as ready to kill as they were to make whiskey. Deputy Marshals Reuben Fry and Otis Wheeler took the stand and identified Franklin as one of the five armed men who had approached them and Trammell at the crossroads near Fancy Hill on June 26, 1888. They testified that they believed it was Franklin and Fayette who had fired one shot apiece at Trammell, one of their bullets killing him. Both lawmen cited Franklin's attempt to locate Trammell in Black Springs and to instigate a gunfight in January of 1888. According to the prosecutors and the two deputy marshals, Franklin obviously had motive and a willingness to kill a federal peace officer.

And when Franklin finally took the stand in his own defense, his defiant nature reared its head. He denied having killed J. D. Trammell. Prosecutor William Clayton asked him again if he had murdered the deputy marshal, and Franklin ignored the question. The Hanging Judge intervened to make Franklin answer and repeated the question once more himself.

Franklin gruffly replied, "No, but I was damned sure a well-wisher to it."

Family lore always stated that he served time in prison for that remark, ruled in contempt of court. But the truth is, the jury rendered a verdict of guilty for conspiracy (to murder) on August 9.[101] It would seem that the court had little appreciation for Franklin's sense of humor.

It might seem strange that Franklin was only charged with and found guilty of conspiracy when the grand jury had originally indicted him for first degree murder. However, the prosecution may have felt they didn't have enough of a case to convict him for murder. Reuben Fry claimed that he saw Franklin and Fayette shooting, but there was no way to prove whose bullet killed Trammell, if either one did. Both deputy marshals, Fry and Wheeler, admitted the whole thing had happened very fast and that the nature of the brush and the terrain had made it very difficult to see anything. The identification of the murderers seemed to come as much from a few locals' opinions about who had done the crime as it did from the deputy marshals' actual observations. Some of the Cogburns would later claim among themselves, dryly with tongue in cheek, that the deputies were too far in back of Trammell and too busy hiding in the brush when the bullets started flying to see anything. What was certain was that Franklin had come up the road with four other armed men and approached known and sworn peace officers in an aggressive, threatening manner. Shots were fired from that group. Whether he had pulled the trigger or not, he was present with those who did. That and his earlier death threats against Trammell were enough to prove beyond a shadow of a doubt to the jury that Franklin had "conspired" to murder. In other words, according to the finding of the jury, he was a well-wisher to murder.

No formal charges were ever brought against Franklin for whiskey charges resulting from Reuben Fry's affidavit in 1888. There was no evidence to link him to moonshining, as he hadn't been caught during Fry's raid, and Trammell was no longer alive to give testimony to the findings of his investigation.

As it was, Franklin was handed over to the jailer and remanded to the U.S. jail. On August 29, he was once more brought before the bench. The Hanging Judge was quick in meting out justice, and by eight o'clock in the morning Franklin had been sentenced to two years in the Ohio Penitentiary at Columbus and a $1,000 fine, plus court costs. On October 3, just two weeks before his first son was born, U.S. Marshal Jacob Yoes delivered him to that correctional facility and handed him over to Warden E. G. Coffin. The outlaw was now a prisoner. Like the song, he'd fought the Law, and the Law won.

10

Four Walls and Steel Bars

Columbus, Ohio, was one hell of a long way from the mountains of Arkansas. The huge brick walls of the prison rose up from the streets of that city like some castle, holding prisoners both from within the state and those taken from abroad on contract from federal courts. Franklin swapped the pine-scented fresh air of Montgomery County for a four-foot by seven-foot cell with stone walls and a steel door. His humble furnishings consisted of a single cot that could be folded up against the wall when not in use.

Except for sleeping hours, he was rarely in his cell. The Ohio Penitentiary, as well as the state, prided itself on the modern prison and the correctional philosophy it employed. The institute was run with the idea that criminals weren't lost causes—or at least that theory was espoused by the administrators. Prisons of the past had always been more about punishment than reformation, but the Ohio Penitentiary, among a few others of the time, sought to change that. Rehabilitating prisoners and preventing recidivism was the chief goal, and it was believed that new scientific concepts and theories could aid in the process.

During admittance, prisoners were subjected to the Bertillon method for identification purposes, which was the latest rage among more "civilized" penal institutions. Using the metric system, the height of the prisoner as well as bone measurements were taken—length and width of head, length of foot, middle finger, etc. The idea was to take enough measurements that criminals couldn't hide behind aliases and rates of recidivism, or repeat offenses, could be tracked. The prisoners were marked by different-colored clothing. They signed a behavior contract promising to obey all regulations. After six months of review, prisoners who played by the rules were given gray and white striped clothes. Those who didn't wore the standard black and white stripes that came to emblemize American inmates prior to the invention of orange coveralls.[102]

All prisoners were required to either work at a trade they knew or learn a new one. They were hired out to contractors and manufacturers to work in the various prison workshops. Piecework could be given to individuals, and in that manner an inmate might make nominal wages for his completed projects. Despite appearances, it would seem the prison officials weren't motivated only by philanthropic and social concerns. The state made money off the sweat of the prisoners' brows, and private businesses made money from steeply discounted labor. If they were lucky, the incarcerated might have a few dollars in their pocket from years of hard work at the time of their release. Franklin's "vocational training" required that he spend his days making brooms. The women incarcerated in their own area of the prison worked at many of the same jobs as their male counterparts, with the addition of laundry duty for the entire facility plus making cigars.

Among the rolls of prisoners were ten wild Apaches, and it must have been a unique sight to see those fierce, stoic desert fighters weaving chair seats.[103] No doubt, neither Franklin nor the Apaches found much practical use for their newfound skills once they made it out of prison. Broom-making and chair factories were in short supply back where they came from.

Prisoners were to go to church on the grounds every Sunday, and the Catholic prisoners had their own large chapel. A lack of education was seen by the prison officials as the root cause of many of the prisoners' crimes, and all inmates were required to attend night school for a few hours every evening. A prison library of some 2,000 volumes was available to all. According to his U.S. census information, Franklin was illiterate before his incarceration, but is listed as being able to read and write in the years after. It would seem that the Ohio Penitentiary's efforts toward the rehabilitation of prisoners, a recent concept in the nineteenth century and still a topic of debate today, did bear at least a little fruit.

Among those incarcerated with Franklin were other men who had been sentenced in Judge Parker's court. A family story has it that Franklin became friends with Eddie Reed, the son of outlaw Jim Reed and the famous bandit queen Belle Starr. Records indicate that Reed arrived at the Ohio Penitentiary on August 1, 1889, just one month before Franklin. He had been convicted of larceny and of receiving stolen goods, which boiled down to simple horse thievery. He was sentenced by Judge Parker to seven years. It is possible that he and Franklin met in the United States jail at Fort Smith during Franklin's time there before his first court hearing.

Reed spent only four years of his sentence at Columbus. His sister, Pearl, always claimed that she became a high-toned prostitute in Fort Smith to gain money for his release. However true that may or may not be, it was she who procured and paid for the high-dollar attorneys who eventually got Eddie a presidential pardon in 1893.[104] Less than a year later, Eddie was charged with introducing liquor into the Indian Territory, but his case was dismissed for lack of evidence. Pearl may have been at work again. She could certainly afford to hire good lawyers—her professional services in the red light district reputedly came at a high price.

Eddie Reed was born a branded man, considering who his parents were, and many of his supporters and friends claimed that he was never an outlaw except in the minds of newspapermen and suspicious lawmen. Ironically, he became an express guard for the Katy railroad and a Deputy U.S. Marshal in 1894. He married a schoolteacher, bought a home, and settled in to his work as a peace officer. One of the little-known tough men of the time and place, he was reportedly hell on wheels with a gun and deadly calm in a fight. He had grown up among some of the most famous and feared outlaws in the Old West, and perhaps he had picked up a trick or two from the likes of the James-Younger Gang or Sam Starr.

In 1895 he faced off against two gunmen on the streets of Wagoner, Indian Territory. Dick and Zeke Crittenden, former Deputy U.S. Marshals, were drunk and had wounded a resident. They were firing off their pistols in the street when Reed approached them. A gunfight ensued, and Reed gunned them both down. On December 14, 1896, he was drinking in a saloon at Claremore and heard that two men, J. M. Clark and Joe Gibbs, were in town. He went to arrest them for selling whiskey. The two outlaws were ready and waiting for him in ambush and cut him down in a crossfire of shotgun blasts at close range.

What was more important about the reforms instituted at Ohio Penitentiary was the parole system that was put in place in 1885. Unlike Eddie Starr, Franklin could expect no presidential pardon. But the new law enacted by the Ohio legislature required that a prisoner only serve the minimum term for his crime before being eligible for parole. A State Board of Pardons was created in 1888. The minimum federal sentence required for a conspiracy conviction was one year. It is not known if Franklin wore the gray stripes of a trustee, but his behavior in the prison must have been satisfactory. After serving a year and a day of his two-year sentence, he was set free by the board.

The train ride back to Arkansas must have seemed like it took an eternity to him. Other than letters, he'd had no contact with Annie while he was incarcerated. His first son, Joe, still just a round belly on his mother when Franklin left, was now almost a year old. Watching the strange man who stepped off the train in Arkansas would be the child's first chance to lay eyes on his father. What's more, Franklin was going home to a land that hadn't changed any since his departure. The moonshining was still rampant in Montgomery County. Franklin knew nothing other than farming, and that wasn't going to pay enough to give his family a decent life. The temptations of easy money making moonshine would be there. The old Devil himself might be waiting on the train depot right behind Annie, winking one coal black eye and smiling at him like a long-lost friend.

11

Going Straight

Many of Franklin's kin had to make trips to Fort Smith while he was locked up. Bill Cogburn, Mike Cogburn, John Barnett, and others had been fined, given short jail sentences, or at least dragged through the expense and difficulty of trials for liquor violations.[105] Jack Hopper had finally arrested Fayette Cogburn on October 12, 1889, little more than a week after Franklin stepped foot in the Ohio Penitentiary.[106]

Fayette's trial was set for November, but when the trial neared he claimed he was unable to afford to bring in witnesses who could prove his innocence. The court issued subpoenas, but it wasn't until the end of November that Jack Hopper could serve the witnesses Fayette had requested. On December 6, Fayette's court-supplied defense counsel and the summoned witnesses tried to paint him as a solid, law-abiding citizen who hadn't even been present when Trammell was killed. Supposedly, he was two miles away and over the mountain at the home of Mike Cogburn, Franklin's uncle, at the time of the shooting.[107] No matter what he claimed, Fayette was found guilty of conspiracy. On December 10, 1889, Judge Parker sentenced him to two years in the Arkansas State Penitentiary at Little Rock, and a $1,000 fine, plus court costs—an identical sentence to the one given to Franklin. Fayette was turned over to the Arkansas State Penitentiary on January 2.[108] It would seem the jury didn't buy his alibi, or perhaps they just thought he, like his cousin, was a well-wisher too.

Franklin's, Fayette's, and Page's jail time had changed things for the family. While the moonshining may have still been going on in Montgomery County, the large-scale operation of the Cogburns had taken a big hit. No longer would they ply their trade with quite the same bold aplomb and daring they had before the deputy marshals started showing up in the mountains in force. If a moonshiner was going to stay in operation, he had to be much more cautious about his still locations and their size, and keeping lookouts posted.

It has been said by the family that Franklin became a different man after his return from prison. He did come back to live in Montgomery County with his wife and they began raising a family. Apparently he was a good father, and his children worshipped him.

In 1895, Franklin was making payments on a farm he had bought in the Scott Township. He also homesteaded another 122-acre piece of ground in 1901, which after five years of "proving up," he received a deed for. According to the Homestead Act of 1862, a homesteader who filed on public lands was required to make some improvements on his new real estate, such as fencing, plowing in crops, digging water wells, or building a home. After five years the homestead claim was replaced with a deed of ownership if the property was thus "proved up."[109]

Franklin was also the vice-president of a local farmer's alliance and was doing everything he could to get ahead in life.[110] The township and country along Polk Creek near the original site of Caddo Cove, or old Black Springs, was a tight-knit community that included the homes of Bill Cogburn, Page, his son

John H., and Fayette's brother Leander. It seems that Franklin had pulled close to those he could count on.

Before Deputy Marshal Trammell was killed, the Cogburns trusted more people. However, many of those they put their faith in—family by marriage and supposed friends—either turned against them or gave damning testimony in court in order to save their own necks. The court's war on the moonshiners hadn't necessarily proved that blood was thicker than water. There were more Cogburns in the county than ever, but the clan began to break up into individual families and their friends. In-laws and neighbors were no longer assumed to be trustworthy before they proved themselves.

Franklin's father-in-law, Joseph Spurling, had looked after Franklin's wife and infant son while he was in prison. Annie's mother passed away in 1900 and Spurling boarded with a neighbor nearby until he remarried in 1908.[111] He no longer practiced medicine and simply helped watch over Franklin and Annie's growing family, which numbered eight children by the time of the old man's third marriage.

Somewhere during these years, Franklin "got the religion," as mountain folks put it. Whether it was a slow process or he attended one of the days-long mountain revivals and came to "know Jesus" like a bolt of lightning isn't known. His step-father, Carter Markham, had been a Baptist minister, and many of the community along Polk Creek were members of the Mount Gilead Baptist Church. His brother Bill helped saw the new logs for rebuilding after the original church burned. The Ouachita Baptist Association's records show that Franklin was a licensed minister in 1909–11, although that is not to say he went soft. Montgomery County still had some rough folks, and a man needed to keep his rifle handy. In the Old Testament hell-and-brimstone fashion, he became a preacher, albeit a gun-packing one, as liable to send a wrongdoer to hell with his gun as to threaten them with it from his Bible.

Many of the original Cogburn Gang may have attended church more regularly, but some of them never quit their moonshining. Fayette eventually did his time in prison, but was fined again for making whiskey in 1894. After a court summons was posted for Bill Cogburn on a big tree near his home, he too found himself back in trouble for dabbling in the manufacture of spirits.[112] Be that as it may, Page's original gang of moonshiners had mellowed some and learned the hard price to be paid when bucking the Fort Smith Law. A smart man would keep a low profile and make just enough whiskey to keep his family in a little extra money.

However, there was another bunch of men in the county that either forgot what had happened to the Cogburn moonshiners or were too young to remember. They became just as bold in their operations and even wilder than Page's gang had been. They too might have gone to church, but didn't believe in turning the other cheek. With the demand for good, mountain-made cat whiskey greater than ever, accusations of stealing whiskey stills and caches led to many a brawl or shooting. From 1900 to 1910, one feud after another erupted among the Montgomery County moonshiners, one of them among the Cogburns themselves.

George Washington Cogburn, known simply as Little George, was a son of Henry Cogburn, one of the three original brothers to come to Arkansas. Henry had moved his family to Texas late in the Civil War, but had brought them back by 1880. He had enough children to be a clan all by themselves. Little George, born in 1871, took up the outlaw business where Franklin left off. He could saw out a mean fiddle at a country dance that would bring all the young folks down from the mountains, or he could play tune with his Winchester if his dander was up.

All hell broke loose at a Fancy Hill picnic on July 25, 1903. Little George vowed that if two of his enemies showed up at the social gathering, "the creek would run red with their blood."[113] The threatened men, Dave Perrin and Jim West, showed up anyway. West was a son-in-law to Little George's brother Andy, and Perrin was the brother-in-law of Bill Cogburn, Franklin's brother. However, this later generation didn't let family connections get in the way of violence. Little George had gotten into a fistfight with Jim West sometime just prior to the picnic, perhaps over a disagreement stemming from moonshining. Little George wasn't a big man, but he was ready and willing for any kind of root-hog-or-die kind of fight. He gave West a beating in their fisticuff match, and that is at least a portion of what led up to the shooting at the picnic in 1903.

There are many versions of the story, depending on which family is telling it. Supposedly either Little George and his brothers Will and Andy, or West and Perrin were running a "lemonade stand" at the picnic. I'll leave it to the reader to surmise what kind of refreshments were being sold and just which bunch was selling them. Vouching for who shot first can still get you in a feud of your own down in Montgomery County, but the upshot was that Little George took his rifle and "did for" both Jim West and Dave Perrin. Little George's descendants claim that West and Perrin showed up to the picnic popping off their guns and shot his hat off to start the fight. Jim West's kinfolk claimed that he wasn't even armed and had his four-year-old daughter in the wagon with him when he arrived.[114] Dave Perrin did have a gun he had borrowed from Bill Cogburn, but his family claimed Little George shot him in the back even after he turned and fled upon seeing West take a bullet in the brisket. Dave Perrin was dead on the scene and Jim West died of his wounds later.[115]

There is an old story that either someone involved in the fight or a bystander ran for his horse to get out of danger. He was so shook up he failed to free his mount from the tree it was tied to. In a wild panic and not realizing he wasn't going anywhere, he whipped and spurred the poor horse while it could only wind itself around and around the tree.[116]

Dave Perrin's father had given Bill Cogburn a home when he was just a long-legged teenage boy without a parent to call his own. Bill had eventually married Dave's sister, the reason he was drawn to the Perrin Home in the first place. He didn't take kindly to Little George putting bullets into his family and let it be known that if Little George didn't turn himself in he would "lay for him" and make a little Winchester justice of his own.[117] Also, Dave Perrin was well liked by many of the other Cogburns along Polk Creek. Little George wasn't afraid of the Devil himself, and the Cogburns split over which one of them to side with. However, either a family council convinced Little George to turn himself in to avoid a bloody feud or he just did it of his own accord. He was eventually convicted of the murder of West and Perrin and sentenced to five years in prison, but apparently there was to be a retrial on some technical grounds.

Many of the clan siding with Bill Cogburn blamed Andy for their friends' deaths more than they did Little George. They felt that Andy had instigated the bad blood that led to the shootings, but he avoided any murder charges. Will Cogburn, the other brother present at the picnic with Little George, was to be tried for murder at Mount Ida. As evidence of just how far the feud gone after West's and Perrin's deaths, on July 3, 1905, Andy Cogburn and a few friends were coming home from Will's trial and were ambushed near the south fork of the Caddo River. Some twenty shots were fired their way, but none of them hit home. As the July 6, 1905, edition of the *Mena Star* reported, "Cogburn [Andy] drew his revolver and returned the shots, it is believed with deadly effect. This fracas is supposed to have grown out of the killing of Dave Perrin and James West in 1903." Bill Cogburn openly plotted the demise of Andy and

Little George among the Perrin family, and perhaps the ambush was of his making. Despite Andy's claim to have killed one of his attackers, no death was reported.

Little George didn't stick around for a second murder trial and a chance at another guilty verdict. He took to the brush, and for the rest of his life he was a fugitive. His eluding the Law has become a legend in Montgomery County folklore. Lawmen could never seem to find him, even when he was in Arkansas. The story is that he hid in an above ground vault or mausoleum in a mountain cemetery, even sleeping there while he waited out those searching for him. My grandfather told how he was once at a Decoration Day at the Cogburn Cemetery at Fancy Hill and spied someone at the edge of the brush. The man had a big mustache and a rifle across his saddle and was keeping a careful eye on any strangers arriving on the scene. He nodded politely to some of the people present, but continued to sit his horse in the timber. My grandfather was a small boy and he jerked on his mother's dress and pointed out the man. She told him that the man was Little George and he was "on the scout," an old-time term for a fugitive from the Law.

In the years that followed, it is hard to tell where the legend of Little George ends and the man begins. There are those who say he killed four or five men in his lifetime, but his family only vouches for three. When things got too hot for him in Arkansas he would go to Texas to hide among kinfolk there. Supposedly, he killed his third man, some say a peace officer, down across the Red River in Cooke County or thereabouts. But according to his family, it was another case of self-defense. Tales of bank robberies, horse thieving, and other killings are said by many in the family to be nothing but fanciful tales. J. C. Whisenhunt, in his multivolume collection of Cogburn folklore published in *The Looking Glass* magazine, attributed several bank robberies and murderers to Little George and his supposed black-hatted, masked compadres, the Lance brothers. But none of them hold water when checked against documents of the period. In fact, the actual culprit was caught and convicted for the same robbery of the Glenwood Bank in 1920 that Whisenhunt pinned on Little George. However, many an outlaw probably got more crimes laid on their plate than they actually ever committed—part of being infamous. Many years ago, there were those among the Cogburns who swore Little George was a sneaky thief and a killer, and there were just as many who swore he was a tough but good man who was simply caught in some bad spots where he had to defend himself.

It would seem that many Cogburns had a nose for trouble and gun scrapes. Andrew Cogburn, of distant kinship, was killed in the famous vigilante feud in Taney County, Missouri when the Bald Knobbers rode wild through the country killing and hanging those who crossed them.[118] Deputy John Cogburn and Roger Mills County Sheriff Andrew Bullard were killed by the outlaw Bert Casey in 1902 along Dead Indian Creek, near Cheyenne, Oklahoma.[119] Also in Oklahoma, Fate Cogburn, World War I hero, was gunned down in his front yard. His attacker rode up to him on horseback while he was talking to his sweetheart. Threats were exchanged and Fate was too slow to get to the pistol in his waistband.

While there were many Cogburns who stayed clear of the rowdy doings of their kinfolk, it goes without saying that some of the family had done much to earn its hard name. Annie Cogburn had long had her fill of the violence in Montgomery County. Sometime prior to 1910 she and Franklin finally moved north to Yell County.

Perhaps their relocation was due to the breach in the extended family over Little George's killing of Dave Perrin or the fact that Franklin's brother and close kin were still making whiskey and running the risk of going back to jail. She didn't want that kind of life for her children. Or maybe it was financial troubles that caused them to move north. The census of 1910 shows them renting a farm in Rover Township, whereas they had owned two farms along Polk Creek in the years before.

The subject of finances brings up other questions about Franklin and his family. The feud that split the Cogburns had one other driving force behind it that had little to do with Little George. Whether it was true or not, many of the Cogburns and others believed that Franklin held a share of the gold that Page Cogburn, and perhaps Franklin's father, John Wesley, had stolen in the raid on Albert Pike's home in 1863. While it is has already been pointed out that Page probably wouldn't have immediately gone and joined the army if he was leaving behind a fortune in gold, that didn't stop people from believing that he had. And as John Wesley was Page's brother, it stood to reason that Franklin might have inherited some of the Pike treasure.

According to legend, Page and his counterparts had found a pot of gold coins stashed under a rock that served as a doorstep into Pike's front door. Page took the lion's share, and those who had helped him split the rest. Considering how poor both Page and John Wesley were in later years, the thought that either of them was holding a stash of treasure seems preposterous. However, envious people's imaginations know no boundaries when it comes to dreaming of pots of gold at the end of rainbows. Adding to the suspicions that some of Page's bunch had cached stolen gold was the habit of hiding money even the poorest mountain folks had. They hid coins under fence posts or buried them most anywhere they thought they could find them again. Not trusting banks, it was a way of depositing and safeguarding their hard-earned and meager savings.

As the treasure tale goes, most of those who raided Pike's home spent their loot in a hurry. Naturally, those who frittered away their cut looked enviously on those who hadn't. None of the clan in later years was even sure who had received a share of the gold, but some of Page's close kin were bound to have a stash of Pike's treasure. Franklin's attempt to go straight was seen as standoffish, and there were those who suspected that his true motivation for separating himself from many of the family was protecting a share of the gold handed down to him by his father. None of the treasure seekers seemed to consider that Franklin's children were just as poor and barefoot as the rest of the kids in the county. It would seem odd that a man with a supposed cache of gold would be living in Yell County on a rented hardscrabble farm, but such realistic considerations don't get in the way of the real dreamers.

Another factor that may have contributed to the move to Yell County was Franklin's failing health. Sadly, he was not long in that county. On April 1, 1912, he died at the age of forty-five. He suffered with what was labeled as pneumonia, and the very same man who had survived shootings, manhunts, and many a fracas died in bed. There is no mention of his having come out of prison with any ailments, but it is possible that he had tuberculosis, which was a common malady of the times. If that was the case, it is sadly ironic that he would die from a form of the same disease that had taken his father at a young age, and both of them infected while in prison.

Franklin is buried in Yell County, near his last home. Although he kept his guns handy, even in his later years, he was never in trouble with the Law again up to the time of his death. However, a postcard written to him by one of his daughters just weeks before his death shows that despite his reformation, he may have had a little bit of outlaw still in his heart. She apparently knew he would enjoy a good fight story and ended her letter with one. Two of her neighbors, Mr. Jackson and Mr. Conley, had a brawl. According to her, *Mr. Jackson hit Conley's nose all to pieces and whipped him. The Law came and turned Jackson over to the circuit court.* Franklin would have understood Mr. Jackson's legal dilemma more than most. Sometimes a man had to fight, but there was always a price to be paid for violence.

Despite Franklin's earlier years at odds with a certain judge and force of lawmen, his tombstone reads, REVEREND JOHN FRANKLIN COGBURN. To his eight children and many neighbors and friends of his later years, he was a good, hardworking, Christian father. Maybe he never was a bad fellow to begin with. Perhaps prison had changed him, or simply the love of a good woman and his faith made him a better man. The dichotomy of the outlaw gunfighter and the holy man might bother some, but I would once again argue that he was simply a man of the times—equal parts good and bad, kindness and wrath and hellfire.

Anna Belle Cogburn was widowed, but Franklin's death did allow her one wish. She was a pioneer in her own right and had seen much in her travels from Tennessee to Minnesota to Arkansas. She had almost frozen to death in Iowa when her family had nothing but dried ears of corn to burn for fuel during a blizzard. She had traveled by wagon and train over miles and miles of prairie and mountains and rivers of countless names following her gypsy father. Montgomery County held both the bitter and the sweet for her. She had seen her man hunted by the Law and eventually laid low while still in his prime. But it was also the land where she had found him and where her sons and daughters were born. But the good things she remembered didn't stop her from dreaming about a new home for her family. Perhaps she and her children inherited that old Spurling itch to see some new country, for they had made up their minds and Arkansas would soon be only a memory for them.

Sometime around 1914 the family loaded up their belongings and moved away. They went west in a wagon train just like the original Cogburns had come out of Tennessee all those long years before. They settled in Leflore for several years and then moved on to Durant before finally landing for good near the town of Clayton, all in the newly formed state of Oklahoma—once the Indian Nations where all outlaws flew. In-laws and other Cogburns and Montgomery County friends went with them and scattered over the countryside. Many of these were allies who had stood with them during Franklin's troubles and sided with them during the feud. There are still Cogburns in Arkansas who will tell you that all the wild, mean, shoot-'em-up Cogburns went to Indian Territory back in the old days, but that isn't exactly true. There were plenty of rough-and-tumble Cogburns left behind when Annie and her brood headed west and left the bloody Ouachita Mountains behind for good.

12

Over the Mountain

Much of Franklin showed in his sons after they were grown. And in their younger years it appears that a couple of the boys, of whom there were three, tried in a small way to imitate Franklin's tough-guy status. They were all tall men, and three of them were enough to tackle just about anybody.

Joe was the eldest, and the finest farmer. He was the tallest at six feet four and might also have been the toughest. In an age when the money for a two-bit Barlow pocketknife was hard to come by for poor folks, he carried a custom-made, lock-blade pocketknife in his pocket for self-defense. Apparently, Joe was as fearless as his father had been, and he was old enough to remember the feuding days back in Arkansas. Sometime in the 1940s he and his family rented a home above the Rock Crusher Hole on the south bank of Jackfork Creek near Clayton, Oklahoma. The house had a notorious reputation among the locals for being haunted, and even the flooded quarry nearby was supposed to have a monster swimming in it that was said to break the heaviest fishing tackle, eat small dogs, and boil the water around swimmers as if about to attack them. The house itself had stood vacant for some time, and more than one renter before Joe had become terrified by the "haints" said to inhabit it and fled to find another home where things didn't go bump in the night.

Joe wasn't easily scared, to say the least. On his first night in the house, he and his wife had just doused the lights and lain down in their bed when a terrible thumping sounded from the ceiling. In the moments that followed they heard the floorboards creak throughout the house as if someone or some spirit was walking upon them. The faint rattle of chains could be heard following the footsteps, and cabinet drawers in the kitchen slammed open and closed. Soon, something began tapping on Joe's bedpost. Your average man would have quickly gathered the family and loaded his belongings into his wagon that very night, but not Joe. He sat up in bed and struck a match. He held the tiny flame before him, squinting angrily into the dark as if the feeble glow would reveal the poltergeist that plagued the house and disturbed his sleep.

"All right, where are you at, you noisy S.O.B.? Show yourself!" he dared the ghosts.

The house went instantly quiet, and Joe went back to sleep without giving another thought to the supernatural events he had witnessed. When his neighbors would later ask how he could stand to live in that house, he would tell them his story and assure them that he hadn't had a lick of problem with ghosts since he had laid down the law to them. Those who knew him in the slightest didn't doubt he'd done what he said.

Guy was fourth of Franklin's children and the middle son. He had Hollywood good looks and a love of the wild country and hunting. Claude was the baby boy and next to the youngest in the family. Like his father, once he had sown his wild oats he became a preacher and a devout family man. Guy and Claude were especially close, and during their young adult years they ran cattle together on Flagpole Mountain, Pushmataha County,

Oklahoma. Having more cattle than they had people to help tend them, they were lucky enough to own a mule that was a hand by itself. They would saddle and bridle the old lop-ear and tie his reins to the saddle horn. In this fashion, the animal would herd and drive cattle like a stock dog with no rider to guide him. The plain little mule with cow sense amazed many disbelievers who came to watch him work.

Tending livestock in the belly-deep bluestem grass of the piney woods by day left plenty of time at night for scandalous behavior more befitting the Cogburn name. The brothers pooled their money and purchased a 1926 Star automobile, made by Durant Motors and an early alternative to the Ford Model T. They caroused about the speakeasies in several country towns in their new horseless carriage. Wanting to appear tough, Claude had taken to carrying a pistol stuffed in the waistband of his khaki trousers. He wore that gun into a local barbershop for all the tamer sorts to see. He was six foot one, but a lean, lanky sort who never owned a pair of britches that he didn't have to cinch in place with a belt around his narrow hips. After getting a shave and a haircut he was too embarrassed to get up out of the barber chair. His pistol had slipped inside his britches and down his leg. He wouldn't get up because he didn't want folks to see him retrieve his gun from down by his shoe after he had acted like he was Pretty Boy Floyd or Clyde Barrow.

My grandfather Claude and his brothers didn't just get their height from Franklin. If nerve is hereditary, they got it in spades. As young men they would drive yearling bulls into a barbed-wired corner of a pasture and take turns roping and saddling them like a horse to try to ride them for fun. Claude was known as a skilled bronc rider, and sometime in the 1920s a Wild West show arrived by train in one of the new Okie towns. While many a circus or carnival had a prize fighter along, that tent show was hauling a bad bucker with them. The traveling racketeers offered a jackpot to anyone who would pay a nominal price and who could ride their outlaw horse without getting thrown. The Cogburn boys put their resources together and paid my grandfather's entry fee. He shortened the stirrups on the old hull the show people supplied as a saddle while his brothers eared the bronc down until he could get aboard. The ill-tempered nag was truly a bad bucker, but was no match for his newest rider. Apparently, that wasn't how the whole process was supposed to go, at least in the carnies' eyes. They didn't want to pay the promised jackpot after Claude rode their bronc to a standstill before a gathered crowd. From the sound of things, there was bit of a tussle and a few bent noses and knotted skulls before the Cogburns made them pay up. The Buffalo Bill wannabes with their bad horse should have known those long-limbed sons of the mountains had inherited more than a little of their daddy's grit.

Guy Cogburn inherited an 1892 Winchester from his grandfather, Joseph Spurling. Even though he had taken a third wife, the old man was quite a rounder and wanderer in his elderly years. He purchased the rifle while staying in Ladonia, Texas. The railroad had brought a boom to the small town, and he was afraid he was going to be robbed and wanted a good gun to shoot anyone bold enough to accost him. The Winchester became his pride and joy, and the family tells how he would come to visit and sit on the porch rubbing his shooter with an oiled rag, as if tenderly stroking his beloved. The rifle eventually was passed from Guy to my grandfather Claude, then to my father, and finally to me.

Many times I heard what a hunter and woodsman Guy had been, and Spurling's old octagonal-barreled .32-20 was his gun of choice for any kind of game, big or small—man-eaters included. Now, even as a young man, I was skeptical of tales that seemed too tall. One of Guy's hunting stories seemed to merit doubt. He was an honest man, but surely even he might pull someone's leg if they were gullible enough to be entertained by a whopper. According to him, he came across a lion while hunting around Bengal, Oklahoma. This wasn't an ordinary, run-of-the-mill mountain lion, but a male African lion with a shaggy mane. Mountain folks love panther stories, but this was surely a story to top them all.

Now, the .32-20 caliber was never designed for shooting dangerous game and just barely had enough punch to kill a deer efficiently in a good marksman's hands. However, Guy didn't let that stop him. He threw that crescent butt plate up against his shoulder and sighted through the deep buckhorn sights before he let the first round fly. Immediately, he wondered if he was carrying enough gun. He didn't know much about African lions, but he was quickly learning that small, underpowered bullets just made them mad. Instead of charging him, the lion retreated to a thicket and Guy said he could see it angrily twitching its tail and hear its threatening growls. Maybe it was his lack of knowledge about dangerous members of the African Big Five or an ethical devotion to not leaving wounded game behind that caused Guy to go in that thicket after the lion. The way he told it, he pursued the lion along the mountainside, shooting it every chance he got to no avail. No amount of lead seemed to faze the enraged creature. The little bullets his rifle fired were just enough to keep the lion from bringing home a charge. In the end, one highly wounded and irate African lion escaped into the woodlands, and one dejected hunter returned home with an empty gun.

My family always swore that Guy told the truth about his encounter with the lion, so I had to assume that in the heat of battle he had mistaken a cougar for an African lion. I admit to having felt ashamed when I encountered a curious newspaper article many years later. Sometime not long before Guy's strange encounter, a circus train wrecked just northwest of where he was hunting. The crash wasn't a terrible one, but several animals escaped from their derailed and smashed boxcars.

All but a few of them were recovered. Wouldn't you know it—one African lion was among the critters that got away. I guess old Guy did try to fetch a lion for supper and left me to eat a little crow for not believing him. Considering his background, I should have known never to doubt him. He wasn't raised to lie or back down from a fight, even when strange, impossible carnivores were involved in the fracas.

Many of the old-timers back in Arkansas used to spin yarns that claimed the last of Albert Pike's gold went to Oklahoma with migrating Cogburns sometime after 1900. None of my family ever saw any gold coin over the years, nor showed signs of fortunes. Oddly, though, Annie never seemed to be strapped for cash in her later years as an unemployed widow. Perhaps she and Franklin had sold their farms in Montgomery County and she had a little money left from those sales—no one knows. However, one of my aunts recalls my grandfather and one of his brothers hiding a gallon mason jar full of coins under the front porch of the house. The coins were silver and not gold, but perhaps the family did haul off a little treasure with them when they left Arkansas.[120]

Franklin and Annie had not only three boys, but five girls also—Laura, Callie, Maggie, Mary, and Ethel. Those young ladies grew into what folks of the time would call "handsome" women. They were lean and tall like their brothers, but with the poise and patience and the quiet confidence of their mother as well. Men will still come from many a mile away to see a pretty woman, and these Cogburn girls soon took husbands and started their own families.

Maybe bold courage and stubborn defiance breeds true. In the years to come those Okie Cogburns would form a clan of their own in a different set of mountains from where they were raised—the offspring of the tall sons and daughters of a bad-man who looked the Hanging Judge in the eye and didn't blink, and the Tennessee lady who tried to tame him.

13

More Than a Little
True Grit

Readers, movie lovers, and fans of *True Grit* have probably already noticed many similarities and personal names Franklin's life and Portis's story have in common. The Hanging Judge and the deputy marshals can easily be explained by a well-researched plot, but the other similarities beg questioning. While Franklin's life in no way mirrors the plot of the novel, it would seem that Charles Portis was aware of John Franklin "Rooster" Cogburn. After all, the author was born and raised in El Dorado, Arkansas, not far south of Montgomery County. He went to college at the University of Arkansas, and in his profession as a newspaper man he was obviously familiar with research and gathering stories.

None of this is to say that Portis stole anything. I can remember being quite shocked upon reading Larry McMurtry's Pulitzer Prize–winning novel, *Lonesome Dove,* and immediately recognizing some of the famous Texan Charles Goodnight's life among other factual and trivial bits of Old West history and cowboy lore woven into the plot. Such usage of real people and events in fiction does not take away from

McMurtry's skill as an author or mean that he purloined the story. You can guarantee that Charles Goodnight never had a whore along on one of his cattle drives, or at the very least one that looked like Lorie, darlin'. Only a wonderful author could make up such stuff.

If indeed Portis's Rooster Cogburn was a collage or a composite of many men of the Indian Territory era he had researched, he must have known about Franklin Cogburn. The personal names he uses in the novel that match Franklin's tale are too frequent to be coincidences. Like Rooster Cogburn, it is obvious that many of his characters have some basis or connection to real people of that time and setting.

Mattie Ross, *True Grit*'s young heroine, several times refers to her maternal Grandfather Spurling. It was this Grandfather Spurling's gold that Tom Chaney stole from her father after murdering him—the event that set her on the vengeance trail. The California gold coins had been a wedding gift for Mattie's parents. Mattie's father, like Franklin Cogburn, had a Spurling as a father-in-law. Thus, the first similarity pops up in the novel in the form of the real man, Joseph Spurling, Franklin's father-in-law, whose name appears on every witness list pertaining to the killing of Deputy Marshal J. D. Trammell.

Who can forget the outlaw, "Lucky" Ned Pepper, played by actor Robert Duvall and then later by Barry Pepper? As a matter of fact, Joseph Peppers was the first man arrested in the original raid on the Cogburn moonshiners by the deputy marshals. Joseph and his brother, Dick, were Tennesseans who migrated from Mississippi to Montgomery County by horseback in the late 1850s.[121] Joseph was called as a witness in both Franklin's and Fayette's trials for conspiracy, and several of the whiskey charges other members of the gang faced. As noted earlier, he was set free by the deputy marshals just before they snuck Bill Cogburn out of Black Springs. Also, it isn't shocking that Peppers's name would be known enough to steal a space in a novel as the namesake of an outlaw? When Joseph and his brother first settled in Montgomery County, the rest of their family decided to live in El Dorado, Arkansas, Charles Portis's hometown.

John Barnett, originally indicted with Franklin for the murder of J. D. Trammell, would appear to have a rap sheet a mile long even before he joined Page Cogburn's moonshining gang. But when reviewing the court records of the Western District of Arkansas, it is difficult to discern if the John Barnetts listed for various crimes from 1874 to 1889 are all the same man. The Indian Territory held a family of Barnetts who were Creek Indians or lived in the Creek Nation. There were several outlaws among them. To make things more difficult, the U.S. census for 1880 lists at least five John Barnetts residing in Arkansas. One John Barnett or another was twice charged and arrested for cattle rustling in the Indian Territory, for introducing two gallons of whiskey into that same country, and for making and selling whiskey in Montgomery County, Arkansas. Those crimes resulted in Judge Parker handing down two sentences of brief imprisonment in the federal penitentiary at Detroit, Michigan, and one six-month sentence in the U.S. jail at Fort Smith.

The John Barnett who rode with Franklin Cogburn was from Tennessee. He had come west with the Cogburns back in 1859 and eventually married one of their daughters. No matter how many of the crimes listed under his name in the Fort Smith court records belong to him, any researcher and fan of *True Grit* will notice a curious detail among the documents for defendants named John Barnett: the names of two of the men called as witnesses and suspects in one of the John Barnett cattle rustling cases, John Quinton and George Moon. In *True Grit,* the two outlaws Rooster held prisoner in the dugout went by the names of Quincy and Moon. Under the pressure of Rooster's interrogation, Quincy chopped off Moon's fingers and stuck a knife in his gizzard. Then Rooster killed Quincy and found one of the Spurling gold pieces in his vest pocket.

There was a Reuben Cogburn in Montgomery County prior to 1900, grandson of Page, whom many people insist on pointing out as an inspiration for Portis's naming of his one-eyed deputy marshal. But he wasn't even born until 1897, a year after Judge Isaac Parker's death. There never was a Deputy U.S. Marshal named Reuben Cogburn, nor any Cogburn who served in the Western District of Arkansas for that matter, other than perhaps as a temporary posse member. There are two different Reubens listed in Franklin's court documents, but the name was a popular one for the time. However, Reuben Macon Fry would certainly fit the bill as a source for that first name being used for Portis's fictional deputy marshal.

Reuben Fry spent many years in the service of Parker's court and under the leadership of two different U.S. Marshals. He was one of the driving forces behind breaking up the Cogburn moonshiners. Like the Reuben J. Cogburn of *True Grit* trying to settle down from his wild life to run his Green Frog tavern, Reuben Fry operated a mercantile at Lake Village, Arkansas, and then in one in Fort Smith.[122] Fry's son Ed became the deputy warden of the Oklahoma State Penitentiary at McAlester in 1909. Unlike some of his fellow lawmen, Reuben Fry wasn't killed in the line of duty. Instead, he lived to the ripe old age of sixty-four and is buried in the Oak Cemetery with several other deputy marshals from the Western District of Arkansas.

Beyond the similarity of names between Franklin's story and *True Grit*, there are other plot points and character names that Portis seemed to take directly from the days of Judge Parker's court and the outlaw era of Indian Territory. The scene where Mattie Ross is knocked into the rattlesnake pit bears more than a little resemblance to an event that happened in 1882.

A horse thief and his young bride had been murdered and her remains were located atop a rocky outcrop in the Arbuckle Mountains in the Indian Territory. The murdered husband's bones had been recovered by the deputy marshal working the case, but when he presented the evidence to William Clayton, the thorough district attorney wanted the girl's bones too. The lawman protested that the cave the girl's remains lay in was full of rattlesnakes, but the prosecutor was adamant that he had to have more evidence. A party was sent back to the cave atop the mountain. The portion of the cave where the decayed body lay contained a deep pit. Given that all the men present had heard that the pit was full of rattlesnakes, it is no wonder that there was only one volunteer to fetch the bones. Posse member Deputy Marshal John Spencer offered to go after the evidence. He had only a lantern to light the way as he was lowered by a rope down into that pitch-black pit. He had no sooner touched bottom than he frantically shouted for his fellow lawmen to pull him back up. Once back on the surface he informed them all that the rumors were true. The bones were there, but the pit was also full of vipers—a lot of them. None of the rest of the group was willing to go down the rope in his place, but after a few moments to calm himself, Spencer summoned the courage to go back.

Slowly, they lowered him into the black void. The deputy could hear the scrape of the snakes' scaled bellies long before his feeble kerosene lantern illuminated them as they slid across the rocks below him in the dark. Once he landed on the bottom again, he hoped to quickly gather the poor girl's bones and clothing in a burlap sack before the rattlesnakes became too agitated. Apparently he was there too long, or the snakes were already maddened from his previous visit. They were soon all around him, oozing out of every crack and crevice, and hissing and rattling their tails. Like Portis's Rooster Cogburn dangling from a rope to rescue Mattie Ross, Spencer pulled his revolver and shot the heads off a few of the vipers—until the concussion of his pistol reports extinguished his lantern.[123] At the very same time his light went out, an especially big snake he'd shot tangled itself around him in its death throes. Most men would have screamed to be lifted up and dropped the sack of bones, but Spencer was a calm, cool type. He tied the dead rattler to his wrist for a joke and kept gathering evidence. He managed to hang on to his load until he was lifted once more out of the pit. He laughed when his comrades jumped back in fear at the sight of the huge snake he untangled from his arm and neck. Maybe the tethered snake carcass was a way to get even with his fellow posse members for being unwilling to go down into that snake pit.

The murdered girl's skull and bones were displayed in the Hanging Judge's courtroom during the ensuing trial. Spencer's bravery helped the prosecutor gain a conviction and resulted in the hanging of the accused murderers.

The setting for Lucky Ned's outlaw hideout in the rocks and the rattlesnake cave where Mattie wound up were also no doubt inspired by Robbers Cave near Wilburton, Oklahoma. The place is now a state park, but the sandstone cliffs and caves on the side of a mountain were once said to be the lair of all manner of thieves, gunmen, and bandits the likes of Jesse James and Belle Starr and others equally famous or infamous. Dates from the Old West and the names of obscure outlaws can still be seen where they were carved into the soft rock at the cave's mouth. The one-time camp and relay station for stolen horses lies not far north and west of Winding Stair Mountain, which plays so prominently in Mattie and Rooster's manhunt.

According to the novel, Rooster, Mattie, and Ranger LaBoeuf traveled "east and slightly south" after leaving McAlester's Store in pursuit of Lucky Ned and Tom Chaney.[124] J. J. McAlester's trading establishment was the beginning of what would later become McAlester, Oklahoma, when the Katy railroad came through, and Robbers Cave is just to the east and a little south of it. Lucky Ned's hideout, according to Portis, is near the crest of one of the Winding Stair Mountains. Robbers Cave actually lies in the Sans Bois Mountains. The two mountain chains run parallel across a wide valley from each other, but travelers as far back as the 1820s often referred to all the mountains blocking passage immediately to the southwest of Fort Smith along the military road to Fort Towson, Indian Territory, as the Winding Stair Mountains. Perhaps Portis wasn't intimately familiar with the terrain of Southeastern Oklahoma or simply liked the way Winding Stair Mountain sounded. Mattie identifies the hideout as being a limestone ledge, but that portion of the old Choctaw Nation is sandstone country.

The cave that gave the park its name is shallow now, but it was once deeper and could have sheltered many outlaws. It was dynamited sometime during the Depression by treasure seekers, but much of the locale's history has survived the ravages of gold lust and time. And interestingly enough, one of the oldest tales about the cave was that a rattlesnake pit was near the entrance. I can remember as a child being warned of the supposed viper den, perhaps to ensure I was cautious while climbing over the maze of boulders and bluffs. However, author and local historian Stoney Hardcastle believed that the rattlesnake pit story went back to Belle Starr's days and wasn't a modern invention.

Tom Chaney, that powder-burned and scar-faced villain who killed Mattie's father and set her on the vengeance trail, is a name that sounds very similar to one certain, honest-to-goodness, real-life outlaw of the Indian Territory. Frank Cheney, a tall-grass prairie cowboy gone bad, had participated in more than one robbery while riding in Henry Starr's gang during the 1890s. In 1893, Cheney, Starr, and four other bandits hit the Bentonville, Arkansas, bank. With $11,000 taken from the safe and six prisoners in front of them as a screen, they came out of the front door to a hail of gunfire. Most of the town had been alerted to the robbery and shot at will at the desperadoes stealing their money. The hostages the gang had marched out the door with pistols in their backs bolted, leaving the outlaws without any shelter. Apparently the captives risked being shot by their captors rather than facing a sure death at the hands of their wild-shooting friends and fellow townspeople. As Henry Starr himself said, ". . . fifteen or twenty men were shooting at us; it was as dangerous to stay with us as it was to run, and those six men just melted like snowflakes in a puddle."[125] Although one of the bank robbers was shot full of holes, all of them miraculously survived the gauntlet of bullets as they fled out of town on their horses. Starr was later of the opinion that $11,000 "was trifling pay for such a desperate venture."[126] Frank Cheney was one of the men who came out of that bank with a money bag in one fist and a blazing pistol in the other. With lawmen hounding them at every jump, Starr's gang broke up. Cheney was eventually killed by a posse in 1894 near Eagletown, Indian Territory.[127]

One other tidbit is worth mentioning during any discussion of that villain Tom Chaney. Although there were many Chaneys in western Arkansas, then and today, Fayette Cogburn's brother Leander was a brother-in-law to a man named Abram Chaney.

Perhaps the most iconic physical component of Portis's Rooster Cogburn was his missing eye. Who can forget John Wayne cocking his head like a hawk to focus his one good eye, drunk or sober? Actually, there was a one-eyed Deputy U.S. Marshal who enforced justice in the Western District of Arkansas. His name was Calvin Whitson, and he rode for the 3rd Arkansas Cavalry during the Civil War until he was mustered out for gunshot wounds received in action that blinded his left eye. He had a Fort Smith doctor remove the damaged orb in 1890 due to health complications.[128] Although he didn't sport a patch, he did wear his hat cocked down over the maimed eye. Readers of *True Grit* will recall that Rooster didn't wear an eye patch himself. That item was apparently an invention of either the screenwriter or the costuming department for the movie.

Cal Whitson was sworn in as a Deputy U.S. Marshal on January 10, 1889, and again on June 21, 1889.[129] Like Reuben Fry, he owned and ran a store for a time. It is said that the death of his son was what led him to seek employment chasing badmen for the Western District of Arkansas.

Billy Whitson, Cal's son, and Deputy U.S. Marshal John Phillips were killed in a gunfight in 1888 while trying to ambush the Creek outlaw Wesley Barnett and two others twenty miles east of Eufaula, Indian Territory.[130] Billy supposedly killed Barnett's brother, but took a fatal bullet himself in the process.

Interestingly, there are descendants of Cal Whitson who claim that a clerk with the last name of Daggett is mentioned in some of the deputy marshal's service records. While those documents and the Daggett name are yet to come to the forefront, if true, they leave another clue as to the trail of research Portis followed to create *True Grit*. Who can forget Mattie Ross's continuous references to her mighty lawyer, J. Noble Daggett?

It is left to the reader to decide if these many connections and similarities suggest tiny pieces of Franklin's story and other real-life events and people seeped into *True Grit*. The more the evidence mounts, the more it would seem that Portis's rascal of a deputy marshal was truly a composite of different men. Perhaps that one-eyed fat man with a penchant for booze and shooting merely owed his name to a certain outlaw from the mountains of Arkansas named John Franklin Cogburn. Regardless, a real Rooster Cogburn existed in the days of lawlessness in the Western District of Arkansas, where steely-eyed lawmen kept their eyes on the skyline for ambush and bad men fought recklessly to avoid the Hanging Judge's noose.

Many times I have stared at the cracked and torn photo of John Franklin Cogburn hanging on the wall in its antique oval frame or fondled the 1892 Winchester handed down to me through four generations by Joseph Spurling. Long before I knew the truth, the hint of a story was there—even through the vague and feathery light wisps of family folklore. In the end, the smell of black-powder smoke was plain, and I recognized the man in the photo. He was my great-grandfather, Franklin "Rooster" Cogburn, with two good eyes and a tale all his own.

Afterword

To all my fellow Cogburns, I'm truly sorry if this book has jerked some skeletons from the closet or has accidentally left the notion in readers' minds that all the old-time Cogburns were heinous whiskey peddlers, outlaws, and ruffians. Such notions would be far from the truth. Because of those very worries I debated for years whether or not to write this book, or if it should be published.

In the process of telling the "interesting" portions of Franklin's life, I have left out many of the kind actions and daily living of his family and the many good people who lived alongside him. A prerequisite for a good story is the exciting or the unusual, especially in anything dealing with the Old West. Raising children, chopping wood, plowing fields, picking cotton, and weeding corn aren't what most readers are looking for.

Many of the Cogburns of Franklin's era were good people, more apt to obey the law than break it. Of the lawbreakers, the majority of them were only moonshiners. Franklin can proudly claim many good citizens descended from him. They are hardworking, honest, middle-class people. In my own family, every one of my grandfather's children went to college, a testimony to the desire to raise themselves up from the hard times the family had endured.

In my mind Franklin was a good man, even if my telling of his story has shown some of his faults. I'm too far removed from that generation to ever truly understand his kind. Many of we Americans have pioneer blood running in our veins and family stories worth retelling, but we can never truly lay hand to the past. How can people used to refrigeration, cable TV, and cell phones ever understand the old days when men were men and the women had to be damned tough to keep them in line? How can people who are used to crossing multiple states on freeways at seventy miles per hour without ever seeing a thing but pavement ever hope to understand what a day's journey was like back in the horse-and-buggy age? Many outdoor types hunt for sport, but what was it like to have to shoot straight when your family went hungry if you didn't? How many of us who have grown up with the availability of 911 emergency dispatchers and police forces a phone call away will ever feel that our wits and weapons are the only thing protecting our lives, property, or family? We romanticize the Old West, but at the same time we are prone to analyze and judge the raw and often violent events of that time with opinions and beliefs far different from those we hope to understand. Can a generation that settles its differences and squabbles with lawyers and files civil lawsuits at the drop a hat ever understand men who dueled with smoking guns over sometimes so small a thing as honor, a blood feud, or proving their courage against their enemies?

A close family friend from down in the mountains of McCurtain County used to tell us a story from his boyhood. Oklahoma became a state in 1907, but remained wild. Things there have always been twenty years behind the times, and horseback robberies were still happening up into the 1920s. This family friend told us how a band of rustlers had come through and stolen several horses. He rode with a party of grown men who trailed the outlaws and found their camp in the dark by the glow of its fire. The kind man I knew in my child-hood, then only a child himself, was ordered to hold the saddle horses while the grown men with him snuck up and surrounded the sleeping bandits. Without a word of warning they shot every one of the thieves in their bedrolls. Come daylight, they buried the bodies and rode home with the recovered stock and not a single look back over their shoulders. Until Mr. Buddy told folks his tale in his senior years, not a word of that night's vigilante events had ever slipped out. Justice needed no explaining.

How are we to understand such old-timers and the life they led or the choices men and women made while scraping out a living in a land that often demanded you fend for yourself? My dear old Papaw, true to his raising, used to tell us that God wouldn't hold it against a man shooting a criminal in defense of his home or family any more than he would if that man killed a mad dog. There are many now, kinder, gentler sorts who would debate that the value of property or one's life does not go so far as the authority to defend them with deadly force. But they didn't live in 1888, and perhaps would change their minds if they had.

In the end, any attempt at history is often nothing more than digging up old graves, figuratively as well as literally, and those who wish may try to identify the bodies. As for myself, all I can say is that I know Franklin Cogburn a little better than before I wrote this book. I make no claims to totally understand him or to know everything about his life. I have made every effort to be truthful, but any errors or omissions in his biography are mine alone. I can only say that I'm proud to bear his last name. And be you a Cogburn or not, I'd like to think that there's a little bit of Rooster in us all.

I'd like to keep writing, but I've got chores to do. The horses need fed, my guns could use a cleaning, and my still needs tending. Times are tough, money hard to come by, and good whiskey is dripping into an almost full jug.

Notes and References

CHAPTER 1

1. The court records and family lore are unclear as to who this "constable" may have been. There is no evidence of Black Springs having a city marshal in 1888. There was a justice of the peace and a few other county-appointed officials. Perhaps Sheriff Golden employed one of them, or simply a local, to aid him.

2. Jefferson County Board of Agriculture, Manufactures, and Immigration, *Jefferson County, Arkansas, Full Description* (C. S. Burch Publishing, 1888), p. 23.

3. The exception for pistols of a size used by the army and navy is curious. It would seem that a Colt or Remington revolver, or any of the other large-frame pistols available at the time, were legal to conceal. Perhaps full-sized revolvers were thought to be large enough to be difficult to hide under clothing and easier for a lawman to spot. On the other hand, the public and lawmakers had certain perceptions and biases even in the 1800s. Standard-sized pistols might have been acceptable defense weapons for gentlemen during the nineteenth century, whereas hold-out weapons such as sleeve guns and derringers were seen as the trademark of gamblers, prostitutes, highwaymen, and other members of the criminal element. Along this

line of thought, pocketknives were okay to be concealed but other edged weapons were not.

4. *Montgomery County: Our Heritage*, Montgomery County Historical Society (1986). An old-timer once told me that he could remember prisoners cuffed to the tree alongside tied-up teams and saddle horses.

5. Circuit court docket, Montgomery County, Arkansas, January 1–February 1, 1888.

CHAPTER 2

6. George Washington's letters, Washington Papers Online, Library of Congress.

7. Patrick Cogburn, John Franklin's grandfather, continued to use the "Cockburn" spelling until well after he emigrated from Tennessee. Sometime between the 1860 and 1870 U.S. censuses he changed to the modern spelling. Some of the Cockburns changed their last name to "Coggburn" and then to "Cogburn," thus confusing genealogists. Both of these later spellings have survived to the present.

8. 1860 U.S. census, Montgomery County, Arkansas; 1850 census, Marion County, Tennessee; survey and work document, Greene County, Tennessee, May 6, 1844; land records of the three counties from 1835–1859. An approximate date of departure can be derived from the sale of Wash Porter's real estate in Sequatchie County, and the party of pioneers obviously arrived in Arkansas in time to be listed on the census there.

9. There were actually four brothers. Robert Cogburn was the only one who stayed behind in Tennessee.

10. 1850 U.S. census, Gap Township, Montgomery County, Arkansas. The family records suggest that James came to the area in 1848, making him one of southern Montgomery County's early settlers. According to BLM records a cousin, John M. Cogburn, had also purchased a land patent to forty acres from the government in 1820 and recorded his choice of real estate in 1855 at Washington, Arkansas.

11. Montgomery County, ArkansasGenWebProject, roots web.ancestry.com. This is according to a statue placed in the town by the Arkansas State Historical Society. Some more recent historians have begun to doubt that the gap in the mountains was the site of de Soto's westernmost exploration and fight with the Tula Indians.

12. 1855 Arkansas map, J. H. Colton & Co., NY, courtesy of Shirley Shewmake Manning.

13. Ibid.

CHAPTER 3

14. Roger H. Tuller, *Let No Guilty Man Escape: A Judicial Biography of Isaac C. Parker* (Norman, OK: University of Oklahoma Press, 2001), pp. 41–52; Glenn Shirley, *Law West of Fort Smith: A History of Frontier Justice in Indian Territory 1834–1896* (Bison Book, 1968), p. 35.

15. Shirley, *Law West of Fort Smith*, p. 209.

16. Tuller, *Let No Guilty Man Escape*, pp. 41–52; Shirley, *Law West of Fort Smith*, p. 25.

17. Shirley, *Law West of Fort Smith*, p. 25.

18. The Osage were pushed out of Arkansas and then a division of the tribe was again moved out of the Arkansas River Valley in Indian Territory to make way for the Cherokees, whom the government had relocated there. In the years to come, they were forced from Missouri and Kansas. There is some irony and a lot of justice in the fact that the land the tribe finally purchased for a reservation was seen by the government to be worthless for farming, but was later found to be rich in oil deposits. The crafty, adaptable Osage wisely negotiated to keep their mineral rights when the Osage Allotment Act of 1906 broke up communal tribal lands to make way for statehood. The Oklahoma oil boom at the turn of the century made many of them rich—at least the ones who weren't cheated out of their mineral headrights by swindlers.

19. Harman, *Hell on the Border* (University of Nebraska Press, 1992); *Fort Smith Elevator;* Court Case Files, Western District of Arkansas, 1876–1890.

20. Court Case Files, Western District of Arkansas, December 16, 1871.

21. This Sam Starr is not to be confused with the one-time husband of Belle Starr who was killed in a gunfight with Cherokee Lighthorseman Frank West. The Sam Starr and Charles Johnson involved in the axe and butcher knife fight were both African Americans.

22. Court Case Files, Western District of Arkansas.

23. Harman, *Hell on the Border,* p. 198; "George Maledon Interview," *Chicago Daily Tribune,* September 25, 1887; *Morning Republican,* April 8, 1872. Although John Bille (sometimes spelled "Billee") was hung at Fort Smith, he is

not to be confused with another Indian outlaw who came later, John Billy. John Bille was hung with two other men on April 3, 1874. Although wild and violent, like many Indians he abhorred the thought of being hung. He repeatedly begged his guards to shoot him in the chest so that he didn't have to make the long march to the scaffold on his execution day. John Billy, a Choctaw, was hung with five other outlaws on January 16, 1890, for the murder of a whiskey peddler in the Kiamichi Mountains near Talihina, Indian Territory. Many books on Judge Parker's days have jumbled the spelling and the names of these two outlaws.

24. Harman, *Hell on the Border,* p. 204. Evans claimed to have assisted Belle Starr's first husband, Jim Reed, in the robbery of Watt Grayson. It was Grayson that Evans claimed to have tortured to gain the whereabouts of the old man's $30,000.

25. Glenn Shirley, "The Osage Terror," *Buckskin and Spurs* (Hastings House, 1958).

26. Frank West and Sam Starr, Belle Starr's second husband, killed each other in a pistol fight at a Christmas dance at Whitefield, Indian Territory, on December 17, 1886. Jackson Ellis shot or killed at least seven men in the line of duty as a Deputy U.S. Marshal or a tribal policeman, including the outlaw who killed Sam Sixkiller.

27. *Fort Smith Elevator,* August 31, 1888, quoting the territorial newspaper *The Chieftain,* Vinita, Indian Territory.

28. Fort Smith Historical Society. The number has grown over the years as researchers continue to uncover new information.

29. *Huntington Hummer Newspaper*, July 5, 1888; U.S. census, Dayton Township, Sebastion County, Akansas, 1880, 1860, and 1850.

30. Johnson, "The Trammell Family Pioneer Trail," *Come Climb My Tree*, Vol. II (self-published, 1997).

31. Grand Jury Indictment of Franklin Cogburn, Western District of Arkansas, August 24, 1888; *Fort Smith Elevator*, June 29 and July 6, 1888; *Huntington Hummer Newspaper*, July 5, 1888; *The Fort Smith Journal*, June 30, 1888. The *Fort Smith Elevator* article mentions a posse of "15 or ? men," but the second number (possibly 20) is almost illegible on microfilm, so I went with the first and lesser estimate.

32. *Fort Smith Elevator*, July 6, 1888.

CHAPTER 4

33. *Montgomery County: Our Heritage*, vol. I, p. 340.

34. The classic Clint Eastwood film based on Forrest Carter's novel, *Gone to Texas*, or its earlier title, *The Rebel Outlaw: Josey Wales*.

35. Records of L Company, 2nd Kansas Cavalry; Bureau of Pensions, U.S. Department of the Interior, 1892, affadavits and forms filed by John Franklin and William Isaac Cogburn for John Wesley's Union pension. It appears that several other neighbors of John and Page went along with them to join up, as their enlistment dates and locations are the same on the records. Thomas Whisenhunt also mentions in his pension affidavit that he joined up and served with John Wesley.

36. Melvin Cogburn, interview by author, June 1998.

37. *Otago Witness,* April 18, 1863.

38. Melvin Cogburn, interview by author, June 1998; Bond, "One Black Pot with a Yellow Fortune," *Old West* (Fall 1970), pp. 18–19, 54–55.

39. Cobb, "Mountain Legend of Albert Pike's Two Years in the Ouachitas," *Mena Star,* April 22, 1939.

40. Bob Brewer & Warren Getler, *Rebel Gold* (New York: Simon & Schuster, 2003) p. 89. Brewer interviewed Melvin Cogburn, a cousin of Page Cogburn and the son of an outlaw and gunfighter who is mentioned later in this work, Little George Cogburn. Most of the treasure hunters base their beliefs either on Melvin's mountain tales, Ida Cobb's 1930s newspaper piece, or Bond's magazine article, "One Black Pot with a Yellow Fortune." A campsite and recreation area in the Ouachita National Forest now encompasses the site of Albert Pike's home. It is said that the Cogburns gave name to the location as it is now called on maps, Albert Pike. The burned, charred shell of Pike's house or cabin is said to have still been standing in the 1930s.

41. James M. McPherson, *Battle Cry of Freedom: The Civil War Era* (New York: Ballantine Books, 1989). The Enrollment Act of 1863 provided a $100 bounty to volunteers, plus any bonuses paid by states or municipalities. Many men took the bounty and deserted, and then repeated the process elsewhere—bounty jumpers.

42. Records of L Company, 2nd Kansas Cavalry.

43. Hancock, "The Second Battle of Cabin Creek, 1864,"

Chronicles of Oklahoma, vol. 39 (Norman, OK: University of Oklahoma Press, 1961), p. 415.

44. John D. Spencer, *The American Civil War in Indian Territory* (Osprey Publishing, 2006). The Ross faction of the Cherokees switched loyalties to the Union in 1862. Despite Confederate promises of better treatment for the tribes should they win the war, many Creeks and Seminoles and a few Chickasaws stayed loyal to the Union from the beginning.

45. Thurman Wilkins, *Cherokee Tragedy* (Norman, OK: University of Oklahoma Press, 1989); John Ehle, *Trail of Tears: The Rise and Fall of the Cherokee Nation* (New York: Anchor Books Doubleday, 1997). Stand Watie was a member of the Treaty Party who signed the agreement with the U.S. government to relinquish the Cherokee lands in the east in exchange for land in what would become the Indian Territory (Treaty of New Echota). These Old Settlers moved west to Indian Territory and northwestern Arkansas while Chief John Ross's faction opposed the treaty and stayed behind. Once the remaining Cherokees were forced west on the Trail of Tears, Ross's supporters systematically assassinated all of those who had signed the treaty. Stand Watie was the only member of the Treaty Party to survive. Years of bitter, bloody partisan fighting followed.

46. It is worth noting that of the 3,000 plus prisoners brought to Camp Ford from this and one other fight in 1864, only one man from the 1st Kansas Colored Regiment is listed on the prison rolls.

47. Bureau of Pensions, U.S. Department of the Interior, 1892, affidavits and forms filed by John Franklin and William Isaac Cogburn for John Wesley's Union pension.

48. Ibid.; Whisenhunt, "Proof of Incurrence of Disability."

49. Ibid.

50. Ibid.; General Affidavit of Carter Markham, 1892; U.S. census, Mountain Township, Pike County, Arkansas, 1880; U.S. census, Sugarloaf Township, Sebastian County, Arkansas, 1870; U.S. census, Colbath Township, Clark County, Arkansas, 1860 and 1850. The 1870 census shows Carter having infant twin daughters and a five-year-old son still at home from his former marriage. Mary Cogburn and Carter were married October 14, 1870, and she died on April 7, 1873. The 1880 census shows Carter as a widower and having another daughter, Samantha, age three. Samantha might be the offspring of Carter's third wife. Perhaps Carter was briefly married between Mary's death and the time of the 1880 census. It would appear that over the years he was married to Lucinda Thompson, Mary White Cogburn, and this mysterious third wife, and was rumored to have married for a fourth time before his death in 1894. The genealogical tracking of such marriages can be extremely difficult. Many women of the time died in childbirth, and it was not unusual for men to be married so many times. However, Carter was reputed to be quite the cad and woman chaser.

51. Ibid.; General Affidavit of Carter Markham, 1892.

52. 1880 U.S. census, Missouri Township, Montgomery County, Arkansas.

53. Letter from Martha Cogburn to her cousin Nancy, December 3, 1881.

54. Enlistment Records, A Company, 1st Arkansas Infantry.

55. "John Barleycorn Exhibit Online," Old State House Museum, www.oldstatehouse.com.

56. "Noted Moonshiners Captured," *The New York Times*, June 4, 1889.

57. Glenn Shirley, *Heck Thomas: Frontier Marshal* (Philadelphia: Chilton Company), p. 95.

CHAPTER 5

58. Author's correspondence with J. D. Trammell's great-grandaughter, Becky Roseman, 2011.

59. *The Fort Smith Journal*, June 30, 1889; *Fort Smith Elevator*, June 29, 1888, June 6, 1888. The last article is related to the reporter by Deputy U.S. Marshal Reuben Macon Fry, one of the three lawmen involved in the shooting affair that ended Trammell's life.

60. Ibid.

61. Montgomery County grand jury indictment, August 24, 1888; Court case files, Western District of Arkansas.

62. *Fort Smith Elevator*, July 6, 1888. Who this Brooks was has been lost to time. Perhaps he was just the leader of another clan of moonshiners and the term "gang" was the newspaper's attempt to add a little color and excitement to their reporting of the story.

63. The *Fort Smith Elevator* lists John Porter as a local, and he may have been some kind of local authority or county appointee at Black Springs. There was a John Porter living in the township who was the grandson of Washington Porter, who had come to Arkansas from Tennessee with Patrick Cogburn in 1859. However, there was another John Porter from Okmulgee, Indian Territory, who served as a Deputy U.S. Marshal during that time. The re-

porter may have been mistaken that the John Porter of the article was a local civilian.

64. Ibid. Fry would make the same claims in a later newspaper article during a failed attempt to indict Franklin and Fayette Cogburn for the murder of Trammell.

65. Ibid.

66. Snyder, *Antebellum Arkansas: Trammell Families* (self-published, 1994) p. 114.

67. All the newspaper accounts are in agreement that J. D. Trammell was buried at Black Springs. However, Caddo Cove was also known sometimes known as "Old Black Springs."

68. The government had determined that the deputy marshals, as federal employees, were ineligible for government rewards. This was despite the fact that the lawmen weren't salaried and were more like contract labor. Judge Parker lobbied the government to change this practice, as his enforcers were poorly paid for the risks they took, and he thought the promise of hefty rewards would motivate them in their pursuit of lawbreakers. He was unsuccessful in his attempt.

CHAPTER 6

69. Shirley, *Law West of Fort Smith,* p. 52. Letter from Dave Rusk to U.S. Marshal Carroll.

70. Fry, Court case files, Western District of Arkansas, July 19, 1888.

71. Indictment, Montgomery County Grand Jury, August 24, 1888.

72. The elderly woman who told this story was only a girl when it happened. She could only remember that Page took along two of his nephews who were also Cogburns and that the event took place not long after J. D. Trammell was killed. Franklin and Bill were Page's only nephews with the Cogburn last name.

CHAPTER 7

73. The date is unknown, but he was living in Montgomery County at the time of Trammell's killing, as he was subpoenaed as a witness in both Franklin's and Fayette's trials.

74. Michèle Tucker Butts, *Galvanized Yankees on the Upper Missouri: The Face of Loyalty* (Boulder: University Press of Colorado, 2003).

75. Perhaps Joseph Spurling was simply a pragmatist who wanted out of prison any way he could manage it. In 1937 Annie saw to it that a 43rd Tennessee Infantry, CSA tombstone marked his grave, but he also drew a Union war veteran's pension for years, as proven by his third wife's government application to keep receiving the payments after his death.

76. In fact, up until the summer of 1865, more of G Company and the soon to follow 1st U.S. Volunteers froze to death or died of disease and severe conditions than were killed fighting Indians.

77. Among the heirlooms left his family by Joseph Spurling are letters he wrote to Sarah Malvina Sharits, dating from February 29 to October 15, 1867.

78. U.S. census, Pine Top Post Office, Morgan County, Tennessee, 1870.

79. U.S. census, Batie Township, Benton County, Arkansas, 1880.

80. John C. Gunn, *Gunn's New Family Physician, Home Book of Health* (Moore, Wilstach, and Baldwin Publishers, 1867). This book was available by subscription only and appears to be an early version of the home remedy books put out later by Reader's Digest and others.

81. J. L. Nichols, *Home Remedies for Man and Beast,* 12th edition, (J. L. Nichols Publisher, 1892).

82. A family photo of him, long since lost, depicted him with his buggy and driver—as remembered by the grandchildren of John Franklin Cogburn.

83. From the recollections of Franklin's granddaughter, Ruby Cogburn.

CHAPTER 8

84. *Bear Mountain Miner,* March 1, 1889. Bill Cogburn's federal court case files are incomplete, and this newspaper article is all that remains to show the results of his arrest during Trammell's raid in June of 1888.

85. Hopper, Completed Writ of Arrest, Office of the U.S. Marshal, Western District of Arkansas, January 26, 1889.

86. *Fort Smith Elevator,* March 7, 1889.

87. *Fort Smith Elevator,* April 1, 1889.

88. Harman, *Hell on the Border,* p. 75.

89. Ibid., p. 74.

90. Maledon went on tour in later years exhibiting trappings

from his days as Parker's hangman. He traveled from town to town with his ropes, a chunk of the original wooden beam the men were hung from, his guns, and other relics. Even during his days as a hangman, he was known to show off tintypes of the famous desperadoes whose necks he had stretched. If he took no pleasure in the executions, he seemed at least to take great pride in his role and duties. Perhaps this is why so many people who lived in Fort Smith looked on him as something akin to the boogeyman or the Devil himself.

91. "George Maledon Interview," *Chicago Daily Tribune*, September 25, 1887.

92. Harman's *Hell on the Border*, a nineteenth-century take on Judge Parker's time on the bench at Fort Smith, and the *Chicago Daily Tribune* interview with Maledon differ on the killing of the escaping horse thieves. Harman claims Maledon shot those three men after his employment at the United States jail, while the newspaper account states he was a deputy sheriff. Maledon did serve for a time as a Sebastian County deputy sheriff. Perhaps he also had a side job as a guard at the jail, or the newspaper reporter wrote he was a deputy sheriff when he actually meant a Deputy U.S. Marshal. During his entire time as a jailer and executioner for Parker's court, Maledon held a commission as a Deputy U.S. Marshal for the Western District of Arkansas. More investigation is needed to confidently answer this contradiction.

93. Harman, *Hell on the Border*, p. 109.

94. Ibid.

95. Ibid., p. 108.

96. "George Maledon Interview," *Chicago Daily Tribune,* September 25, 1887.

97. *Fort Smith Elevator,* April 3, 1889.

CHAPTER 9

98. Subpoenas, Office of the U.S. Marshal, Court case files, Western District of Arkansas, June 27 and July 15, 1889.

99. *Fort Smith Elevator,* "Their Last Day," "Horses for the Fair," August 9, 1889. Although many references cite August 30 as the day of execution for Jack Spaniard and William Walker, the newspaper obviously felt that August 9 was to be their last day on earth. The paper states that citizens of the city would notice dummy bags hanging from the ropes on the scaffold in preparation for the hanging to take place at high noon on August 9, 1889. A stay of execution may have been granted, delaying the events until the end of the month.

100. Tuller, *Let No Guilty Man Escape,* p. 67.

101. Case #2617, U.S. vs. Franklin Cogburn, Court case files, Western District of Arkansas, August 29, 1889.

CHAPTER 10

102. Henry Howe, *Historical Collections of Ohio: An Encyclopedia of the State,* Vol. I, Ohio Centennial Edition (State of Ohio, C. J. Krehbiel & Co., Printers & Binders: 1888, 1902), p. 645.

103. Ibid.

104. Glenn Shirley, *Belle Starr and Her Times* (Norman, OK:
Oklahoma University Press, 1982), p. 252.

CHAPTER 11

105. Jason Michael Cogburn, or Mike, was Page and John
Wesley's baby brother. Although his uncle, Mike was
only six years older than Franklin.

106. Writ of Arrest, Court case files, Western District of Arkansas, U.S., October 12, 1889.

107. Case #2617, U.S. vs. Fayette Cogburn, Court case files,
Western District of Arkansas; *Indian Citizen,* December
14, 1889.

108. It is unknown just how much of his sentence Fayette
served, as the prison records only show his incarceration
date.

109. U.S. census, Scott Township, Montgomery County,
Arkansas, 1900; Certificate of Registry, land records,
Montgomery County, Arkansas, August 10, 1906. The
homestead claim consisted of 122.57 acres of former public domain. According to the Homestead Act of 1862, a
homesteader was required to make improvements on the
land, and if the property was thus "proved up," after five
years the homestead claim was replaced with a deed of
ownership. Many of the early settlers of Montgomery
County simply squatted on available land, as getting the
deed to a homestead claim would have resulted in them
having to pay real estate taxes. Some of the Cogburns
purchased tracts of land, as did Franklin's grandfather,
Patrick. As the countryside became more populated after
1900, many of the Cogburns began to file homestead

claims on timber land they could have had fifty years earlier.

110. The alliances, similar to workers' unions, were an early American labor movement. The local farmers' alliances were usually branches of the various national organizations attempting to combat what they saw as big business's stranglehold on farmers and commodity prices. While the national offices lobbied for legal and financial reform, the local alliances formed and ran grain cooperatives and stores in an attempt to break up corporate monopolies. Among Franklin's possessions is a ledger book listing alliance officers, entries for co-op corn and cotton yields, and a mechanical stamp and seal officially labeled as the "Montgomery Co., Polk Creek, Farmers' Alliance, #23."

111. His third wife was Mary A. Strawn, a widow who herself had survived two other husbands.

112. Transcript of an oral interview with Effie Vaught, Bill Cogburn's sister-in-law and the sister of Bill Perrin, victim of George Washington Cogburn's gun.

113. Ibid.

114. As told by Effie West, Jim West's daughter, present at the time of the shooting. Her reminiscences were related to me by her son, Ken Billingsley.

115. State of Arkansas vs. George Cogburn, 1903.

116. J. C. Whisenhunt, "Missouri Township; The Lawless Years," *The Looking Glass*, vol. 16, p. 25. Although it is humorous and a good match for the story of the shootout, I've heard similar tales over the years of a scared man trying to ride off on a tied horse.

117. Transcript of an oral interview with Effie Vaught, Bill Cogburn's sister-in-law and the sister of Bill Perrin, victim of George Washington Cogburn's gun.

118. "The I. J. Hayworth Story," *Whiter River Valley Historical Quarterly,* vol. 9, #3 (Spring 1986). The Bald Knobbers, mostly former Union men, were organized in 1865 to end the bushwhacking and murders in Taney County. Before long, the vigilante phenomenon had spread to adjoining counties, and white-hooded men were riding at night and threatening and killing those supposed criminals on their wish lists. The vigilante acts soon transformed into a feud between those who had supported the North and those who had supported the South in the Civil War. Nineteen-year-old Andy Cogburn was one of the Anti–Bald Knobbers. Nat Kinney, the leader of the Taney County Bald Knobbers, gunned Cogburn down in front of a church at Forsyth, Missouri. Like a lot of the Bald Knobbers' victims, Cogburn's death was termed "self-defense." As a side note, Nat Kinney was going to preach that very day at the church.

119. Ken Butler, *Oklahoma Renegades: Their Deeds and Misdeeds* (Gretna, LA: Pelican Publishing Co., 1997), p. 163.

CHAPTER 12

120. My family seemed to have a penchant for hoarding coins, no matter how poor they were. I can still remember the two coffee cans of silver coins my grandparents kept stashed as their private little savings account. However, this practice wasn't that unusual because many people who had survived the Great Depression placed little faith in banks or the long-term value of paper money. My

grandfather sold some cattle in the late 1940s and he and the buyer counted out the purchase price in silver on the tailgate of a wagon. My father, as a small boy, was playing in the wagonbed when it happened. Interestingly enough, many of the coins were quarters. The cattle buyer was a local whiskey maker. Most moonshiners of the day charged two bits (a quarter) to fill a glass pop bottle with white lightning.

CHAPTER 13

121. *Montgomery County: Our Heritage.*

122. Joseph Bradfield Thoburn, *A Standard History of Oklahoma,* vol. 3 (American Historical Society, 1916), p. 1052.

123. Harman, *Hell on the Border,* p. 243. Stories of rattlesnake pits abound in the mountains of Oklahoma, Arkansas, and Texas to the very day. The snakes are said to gather for hibernation during winter or for mating. I myself have seen large concentrations of Eastern Diamondbacks, or coontails, in the rocky ledges and boulders of southeastern Oklahoma, but can't give a scientific reason for their numbers.

124. Charles Portis, *True Grit* (New York: Simon and Schuster, 1968), p. 167.

125. Henry Starr, *Thrilling Events: Life of Henry Starr* (Creative Publishing Co., 1982). Henry Starr's autobiography was written while he was serving one of his stints in prison.

126. Ibid.

127. Some sources claim that Frank Cheney met his end at the

hands of a posse in Texas. Regardless, he died a desperado's death.

128. *Fort Smith Elevator,* June 6, 1890.

129. Court employee database, Western District of Arkansas, Fort Smith Historic Site.

130. Ken Butler, *More Oklahoma Renegades* (Gretna, LA: Pelican Publishing Co., 2007), p. 21.

Beyond *True Grit*

From Brett Cogburn, the great-grandson of the real Rooster Cogburn, iconic hero of the Old West, comes a novel that adds an exciting new chapter to the legend of the Texas frontier.

The Texas Panhandle of the late 1880s is the last great open range of American myth. Into that wild, unknown country ride two young cowboys. Nate Reynolds is the scion of a well-to-do family who lit out for the Panhandle in search of adventure—and gold. Billy Champion is a handsome, devil-may-care ne'er-do-well with a mulish streak and an eye for the ladies. Together they aim to rid this violent territory of rustlers, horse thieves, vengeful Cheyenne, and the rest of the murdering devils who slaughter innocents with no remorse.

But when these two close friends fall for the same green-eyed beauty, their brotherhood will be put to the test. For in a land where the weather, like your fortunes, can change at the cock of a hammer, a man has to stay on his guard if he's going to protect what's rightly his—and live to enjoy it.

In his gritty, pounding debut novel, Brett Cogburn, author of *Rooster: The Life and Times of the Real Rooster Cogburn, the Man Who Inspired True Grit*, proves he's equal to the task of writing the next Great American Western.

Turn the page for an exciting preview of

PANHANDLE

by Brett Cogburn

COMING SOON

Introduction

The greatest thing about stories of the Old West is simply a matter of sheer space. No tale seems too tall under the scope of that big, wide-open Western sky. There is room to let your mind wander along buffalo-scarred trails and up wild rivers that lead to the fossilized and bleached bones of a land that once was, but forever lives on. That mythical West has a flavor like no other, with a grit and a physical feel to it as sharp as the frigid bite of a blue norther blowing down across the plains, or the scorching heat of a desert sun. It was a wild, raw land in an era where everyone seemed tougher, and there were things worth fighting for. Its stories are best told by the light of a campfire or with a far horizon in sight. An old pioneer heart beats strongly in some of us, and we long for a place yet undiscovered.

I had the fortune for many years to make my living from the back of a horse, where cowboys still step on frisky broncs on cold mornings and drag calves to the branding fire on the end of a rope tied to their saddle horn. Growing up around ranches, livestock auctions, and backwoods hunting camps filled my head with stories. My great-grandfather on my mother's side was a former U.S. cavalry sergeant who used to set me on his knee and tell me stories of chasing Pancho Villa in Mexico. His wife told me how she came to Indian Territory in a covered wagon prior to statehood, and how their milk cows got so sore-footed on the trail that they had to shoe them like work oxen. There were family tales of a great-great-grandfather who was a Johnny Reb turned Galvanized Yankee, sent west during the Civil War to fight the Sioux in Minnesota and the Dakotas.

While other children were dreaming of robots and caped superheroes I was fighting Indians and grizzlies with my BB gun on a frontier no one else had ever trod. I dreamed of a place and time where nervy people could throw down their old lives and strike out toward the setting sun.

Perhaps no other thing had a greater influence on my fascination with the Old West than the family stories that went with an old sepia photograph hanging on the wall of my childhood home. My great-grandfather, Franklin "Rooster" Cogburn, was an Arkansas and Indian Territory badman who had a scrap with Hanging Judge Parker's deputy marshals. He was too tough to die and as wild as the rugged mountains that reared him.

And maybe after all those years I've absorbed a little of that Western flavor, like an old piece of barn wood soaking up rainwater. If my tales leave readers with a little taste of trail dust in their mouths, the smell of powder smoke in the air, and the feel of a prairie wind tugging at their shirts, then I'm a happy man. I'll prop my boot up on the fence and spin you another yarn.

—BRETT COGBURN

Prologue

Reynolds Ranch, Higgins, Texas—1936

It's a damned shame, but the Texas I knew is just about gone. Soon, there won't be even a hint left of those days other than the prattling of old-timers with wandering minds and stooped backs, their rheumy eyes twinkling with yesteryear. If we don't die young, maybe that's how all of us end up—nothing more than a story we keep telling ourselves, over and over.

There are folks who call me a pioneer, whatever that means. Those who say that are newspaper writers and such. Mostly, they weren't around to live the life I knew, so they naturally think the old days were something special. Maybe they were, because I miss those years more and more, hard times and all. To hear them talk, I moved out here before the buffalo, but that ain't nowhere near the truth. I was a relative latecomer to this country, but I did ride into the Panhandle before barbwire, railroads, and farmers busted things to hell. The boys used to call me "Tennessee," and we cut a wide swath through this country once upon a time.

Nowadays, most mornings I wake up feeling older than Methuselah. I can't ride a horse anymore, but I still saddle mine up every morning and tie him to my yard fence like I've got somewhere to go. I still tug on my boots even though my achy knees creak and protest, and I'd feel naked without a good hat on my head even if I don't make it any farther than the spur-scarred rocking chair under the shade of my front porch. I'm just old whether I like it or not, but my story is that of a young man in his prime, wild and hard to handle, and yet to learn that life charges a price for every pleasure.

I still don't claim to be much wiser than I ever was, but I do know one thing for sure. Two cowboys getting hold of a race-horse is like children playing with matches. Throw a pretty woman into the mix, and somebody's bound to get burned. Looking back down the long years, that isn't exactly how it was. The horse was just an excuse for adventure, and the woman, well, she had everything to do with our trouble. But hell, I'm getting ahead of myself. . . .

1

Anyone who feels sorry for an Indian hasn't ever been shot at by one. I was a far cry from being an expert where Indians were concerned, but I guarantee you I was learning by the minute.

We ran our horses breakneck across the prairie, with those Cheyenne shooting at us every step of the way. I lay low on my horse's neck, cracking my rope on my chaps leg and urging on the wild-eyed herd of stolen horses before me. Some four hundred yards behind me was a whole passel of the savages, screaming like banshees and whipping their ponies furiously in an attempt to run us down. Here and there, black powder smoke blossomed, and the dull boom of a gun sounded across the prairie. They were way too far off to hit anything from the back of a running horse, but they had their mad up and continued to bang away like it was the Fourth of July.

Occasions like that one led a man to thinking about the ramifications of his actions and the pattern of his life. Right about then I was thoroughly disgusted with my life in general and was promising myself to reform all my bad habits. It was at that moment that I swore off horse thieving and any more dealings with mad, bloodthirsty Indians.

Fast wasn't fast enough to suit me, but he didn't have anything extra to give. He wasn't going to last much longer, and I knew I was just about two jumps ahead of becoming buzzard bait.

To the north, an immense black wall of clouds spread across the horizon, silhouetting the buttes and canyons of the Canadian River. Lightning laced the sky with jagged brilliance. The herd of horses pounded over the rough ground, and the drum of their hoofbeats and the thunder that rumbled from the storm throbbed in my chest like maddened war drums. The dust boiled up in a thick veil, and I felt alone in the insanity of it all. I was caught between a rock and a hard place. I was running blind away from one storm and into another, and I was more alive than ever.

A bullet whistled by me, and it was entirely too close. Those heathens behind me were dead set on collecting my hair. That was the terrible thing about Indians—they had peculiar notions about how one should go about killing one's adversaries. It just wasn't civilized at all the way they went about things. A white man would just kill you, content with the fact that you were dead, but an Indian liked to kill you slow.

They should have made doctors out of the Indians considering how they liked to remove things from the human body. They would cut off and cut up things that most folks naturally take for granted. I was determined that if they were going to catch me, they were going to have to run one hell of a race because I was fond of all my parts. I found the notion of going around missing vital components to be highly unsettling, to say the least. The loss of my scalp, my skin, or my nutsack was among the things that I considered especially bothersome.

Where in the hell is Billy Champion?

Life has taught me that there is no such thing as easy money.

I cursed myself for the stupidity of letting him talk me into such a predicament. It had sounded easy enough, just round up a few Cheyenne ponies one evening and slip them off in the night as easy as you please. Never mind the fact that those same Cheyenne might not be as high on the idea as we were. We had stirred up a hornet's nest is what we had done.

The rain started to fall in huge, scattered drops that popped on my hat brim. One of the horses before me stumbled and fell, followed by the crack of a rifle. I reined away from the crashing animal, barely missing going over the top of him. The shot had sounded pretty close, and I took another look behind me.

Most of the Cheyenne had fallen back some, but one of them, better mounted, had closed to within seventy yards of me. His heels drummed madly against his horse's sides, and he was close enough that I could see the fury beneath the war paint on his face. His rifle wobbled crazily as he strained to draw a bead on me.

Another bullet thumped the ground just behind me and I drew my pistol. My horse lunged with irregular strides, rising and falling over the gullies and rolling ground. I looked down the long barrel of my Colt at the Cheyenne brave bobbing in and out of my sights, and I slowly tightened my finger on the trigger.

Before I could shoot, the Cheyenne's horse lost its footing and cartwheeled end over end. That Cheyenne buck sailed through the air with his arms outstretched, his back arched, and his eyes as big as saucers. I swear he bounced at least three times when he finally hit the ground. He was a rolling ball of dust with an arm and a leg sticking out here and there.

Most of the starch was knocked out of him when he rolled to his feet, and he didn't look so scary anymore. His rifle was gone, his body covered in dust, and his hair reminded me of a mad porcupine. Staggering in a circle, he tried to remember which end was up. His eyes focused drunkenly on me as I rode

168 / Brett Cogburn

away. In exasperation, he sucked up a big breath and tried vainly to blow the eagle feather out of the way that dangled limply in front of his face.

I squalled like a bobcat and raised my pistol barrel to my hat brim in a mock salute. He threw up one hand, middle finger upraised, in a universal and vulgar symbol. It didn't take any Buffalo Bill to read that sign. *Now, where in the hell did a savage learn that?*

One moment I was laughing and the next I was falling. I had one instant of awful recognition as the herd vanished before me, and then my horse was sailing over the edge of a high cutbank. My heart rose up in my throat as I prepared to meet the impact rising up to meet us. We landed in a shower of rock and sand, and when I say it jarred me to the teeth I'm not exaggerating one bit. It was at least a twelve-foot drop, but like many of those range ponies, mine was tougher than nails and he hit the ground running.

I scanned the hill above me where the plain fell off into the deep breaks of the river bottom. A big rifle boomed, and I saw the bullet strike the hill. A Cheyenne there jerked his horse up hard just as another shot stung him with dirt. The brave tucked his tail and fled back over the rise and out of sight.

Thunder clapped, and the bottom dropped out of the bucket. The rain fell in an almost impossible sheet of water. The herd turned toward the river at a wide, flat spread of sand, and I could just make out somebody riding at the lead. I ran my horse by the mouth of a small canyon where a man stood there on its lip, shooting back the way we had come. I thought it was Billy.

The horses hit the shallow crossing at a dead run. Water splashed high, and their legs churned in the deep, sandy bottom. My horse bogged up to my stirrups, but somehow he lunged free and hit the center of the river channel where the footing was firmer. The herd was already coming out on the far bank, where they turned west and raced along the river. I tried to find Billy behind me, but couldn't see anything for the storm.

It was a full hour before sunset, but it turned pitch-black in a matter of minutes. Great gusts of wind brought with them a scattering of hailstones, and I hoped I wasn't about to be sucked up by a tornado. Here and there, lightning lit up the canyon for an instant, but all I could see was rain. The little Cheyenne horse I rode was played out and nickered pitifully for the herd, but there was no answer. I walked him blindly up and out of the canyons, hoping I was following and not at all sure I hadn't lost the trail. *Where the hell is Billy?*

Like the Devil, you mention his name and he pops right up. I stopped in the mouth of a gully leading up to a long rise. The dark shape of a horseman sat crossways on the trail above. It was Billy, and if I looked as bad right then as he did, I was a sorry sight.

Many years later, I saw a book about Billy with a picture on the cover showing a masked man with a smoking pistol in one hand and a pretty woman in the other. They sure made it look wonderful. In the spring of 1881, sitting on a horse with the cold rain running down the crack of my ass, fifty stolen ponies lost in the night somewhere before me and a pack of mad Cheyenne somewhere behind me, I pondered those types of romantic notions. Adventure can be more fun to tell about afterward than the actual experience of the moment.

I rode up to Billy and he was smiling, if you can believe that. He was grinning like a possum, and there wasn't any pretty woman to be had, nor any gun to be found that would smoke on a night like that. I thought about shooting him.

"Reckon the rain will wipe out our tracks?" I sputtered.

Billy looked over his shoulder back down the canyon. He spat out a mouthful of the water running off the bridge of his nose and grinned again. "I just wonder if Noah will have room on the boat for a bunch of Cheyenne nags and a couple of sinners."

"The trick will be loading those wild devils two by two when he comes paddling by."

"Won't be any job at all for good cowboys."

"You reckon Andy's still in front of them?"

"He's living it up right now if he ain't dead. That boy doesn't seem to know that a body can break their damned fool neck running a horse in this. Coming down off the lip of that canyon back there, it was so rough I didn't know if this pestle tail was bucking or falling with me." Billy shook his head as if he really gave a lick about personal safety.

I kicked my horse on up the caliche trail. "Let's hope he checks them this side of Kansas. That boy rides like a drunken Injun."

"Don't worry. His horse is bound to fall over dead before too long," Billy called out as he spurred his horse past me.

I had to over-and-under my horse with my rope and punch the worn-out little devil with both spurs to keep Billy in sight. We caught up with the horses about four miles up where they were scattered out along the banks of a good-sized creek. They were a sorry sight, heads down, asses to the wind. The creek before them was rolling out of its banks. Andy wasn't to be found.

"I had hoped to bed down in Texas tonight," Billy muttered.

"That little grove of trees yonder looks accommodating enough until that creek slows down."

Billy nodded. "I guess these ponies ain't going anywhere tonight, and maybe Andy will show up."

Our saddle horses were done for, and we drifted to the herd to catch new mounts. Only a few of the horses so much as scattered before me—they were that tired after their long run. I started to attempt to pick a good one, but deemed it an impossible feat and managed to rope the first one within my reach. It was a wonder my rain-soaked rope didn't knock that poor little fellow down, as it must have weighed twenty-five pounds.

The little horse came along easily enough, and I laughed as Billy came dragging his choice out by his saddle horn. His victim was set back on the end of the rope and shaking his head. Billy's saddle horse leaned into the pull, but stalled out after a step or two. It was just about an even match. Billy managed to face his horse up and waited until the little paint he'd roped reared high and lunged forward to stand snorting and spraddled on quivering legs. At that, the bronc seemed to have enough and came along willingly.

"Ever notice how a horse will handle like a baby for a hundred pretty days straight, and then when it's muddy and wet, and blowing or snowing, they want to wrestle?" Billy asked. "Never try to catch your old gentle saddle horse in a muddy lot with your Sunday best on, I guarantee you."

"It's just that they ain't any happier than the rest of us with inclement weather."

"What the hell is 'inclement'? Where did you get such a god-awful word?"

"You just ain't got any education, that's the problem with you. This here"—I raised a finger to the sky—"just about fits the bill. Inclement I'd say it is."

Billy had managed to coax the paint up beside him, and as I raised my hand, the bronc bolted and snatched to a halt at the end of the rope. Billy's horse staggered in the mud, the rope digging into Billy's thigh. For a moment I thought his saddle would roll, broadside like he was. He righted things and managed to bring the paint back in, blowing like a buck deer and rolling his eyes.

"Serves you right for roping a pinto."

"That sore-footed nag you've got won't go five miles to-morrow. Besides, I like a horse with some flash." Billy wasn't lying. He loved nothing more than parading around on a good-looking horse.

"Well, I won't have any problem riding this one, will I? You can do all the trick riding you want, and if those reservation savages catch up to us, they might spot you first and leave me alone," I answered as smugly as a cold, saturated man with no sleep in two days could.

Billy stepped down under the trees and began unsaddling his horse. He was silent for once. I was sure I had bested him, and that was enough to make things a little bit bearable.

Billy somehow managed to saddle the paint without a wreck and turned the other horse loose. He had the little fart tied to a tree and hobbled by the time I finished my own. If he hoped to soak some of the devil out of that paint, he was sadly mistaken.

I pitched my roll on the highest, driest spot I could find—one with only three inches of standing water—and flopped down. I could hear Billy splashing around somewhere behind me. I rolled up in my blanket, hoping to sleep or float through the territory, one or the other.

"Riding with you is like riding with my mother. Hell!" Billy grumbled.

"Go to sleep. The rain's slacking off."

"Yeah, it's falling straight down now, and not sideways like before."

April in the Panhandle isn't exactly tropical, and that rain was cold enough to chill beer. It's amazing the conditions a man can sleep under when he's been in the saddle for two days straight. Just before I dozed off to one of the most miserable bed grounds of my life, I asked, "Reckon Andy's all right?"

"Hell if I know."

2

Andy showed up the next morning and I guess you could say he was all right. He was caked with mud from head to toe, his hat missing, gamely half carrying, half dragging his saddle along in his wake.

"I was hoping you boys had some coffee on," Andy said in his squeaky voice.

"We were just fixing to chop up the ark and burn it when you walked up." Billy was trying to wring the water from his blankets.

"Fine horse you got there." I pointed at Andy's feet.

"He quit me."

"They seem to do that to you."

"The son of a bitch stopped in his tracks and sulled up. I couldn't move him for anything. He finally fell over on his side, and I tried almost everything to get him going again." Andy flopped down on his saddle and scratched his scrawny whiskers thoughtfully.

"I like to have never dug my saddle out from under him," he added.

"He might get back up and come trailing in later," Billy said.

"No, he won't," Andy said forcefully.

"I admit you know something about wind-broke, rode-down, sulled-up horses, but you could be wrong," Billy threw back at him.

"No, I ain't."

"How's that?"

"I shot him, that's why!"

"You sure ain't a lover of animals, Andy," I said.

Andy Custer might have been sixteen, although he claimed to be older. He was just short of six feet tall and rail thin. He was blond and fair as white linen. He wore a thin mustache and goatee that he claimed to have patterned after a picture of General Custer he saw once. He had a voice that tended to get higher and squeakier the more excited he became.

Andy fancied himself a sure-enough desperado. You didn't have to ask him because he'd tell you without your asking that he was a bad man—hell on the men who crossed him, and worse on the women who dared to love him. He had a habit of always pulling out his pistol and playing with it when he was sitting around. Billy and I wondered which he played with more, his gun or his pecker.

Andy's image of himself might have been shattered if he could have seen himself then, sitting there muddy and shivering, with his hair sticking out every which way. He idly played with the flopping sole of his right boot, and his big toe poked out of a hole in the other.

None of us had much in the way of clothes, and we were a ragged lot. Our hats were the best, our neckerchiefs were of silk, and our fancy-topped boots were too fine to walk in. But in between, we were mostly just faded rags. My own shirt had so many holes it looked like somebody set me afire and put me out just before it all went.

Now, Billy was as opposite from Andy as could be. He had

a way of looking good no matter what. Even in his rain-soaked rags, he somehow stood out over us. He always seemed to find a way to spruce himself up a mite. I don't know when or where he did it, but he did. That morning he had shaped up the brim of his hat a little, and he had dug a fresh red silk wild rag from somewhere in his bag. It beat me, but it was dry, and so was the white shirt he'd donned. He always had to have a white shirt. It may have been stained and patched, but he looked like a thousand dollars compared to Andy and me.

Some men just have a way about them. Billy Champion had that way. He did everything bigger, faster, and wilder than anyone I ever ran across. I guess that is why I followed him in the spring of '81. I've heard men say that he was a man's man, whatever that is. I know horses and women liked him to uncommon extremes, and he liked them with equal enthusiasm.

There are a lot of stories about Billy, and you can believe what you want. Billy was like that; he made people talk. Billy Champion's downfall was that there wasn't any "back up" in him. He was double-bred stubborn. I loved him to death, but men like him can be hard to ride with because you will get your nerve tried from time to time.

Billy was coal black–headed and a little on the dark side. I always figured he had some Indian in him, but he'd have shot me had I said so. On the worst morning, I never saw him go unshaved, and that morning was no exception. Billy was always an early riser, and while I sat rubbing the sleep out of my eyes and studying Andy, Billy was already done with his morning pruning.

Striding over to me, Billy sat down on a deadfall log, pulled out his ivory-handled Colt, and began wiping it down with a rag and a little can of oil. He always kept his shooter clean. Me, like a lot of other boys I knew, I never took much care of mine. Hell, my old Colt would have probably jumped up and run off in shock if I ever showed it a single drop of oil.

A friend of mine, on a drive to Kansas, once stopped to shoot a cottonmouth on the banks of the Red River. He found his pistol was so rusty he couldn't even cock it. It was locked plumb up. He chunked it in the water, waved good-bye to the snake, and rode off.

A lot of the boys were like that. Most of them just carried them for show or because they thought a man was supposed to. The trouble was, when the majority of the boys on the range carried guns and were apt to settle their differences in the most violent and informal ways, there was bound to be a number of gents who didn't carry a gun for show. Nobody ever said that Billy carried his for show.

Billy wasn't a big man. He might have been five nine or so and didn't weigh more than 150 crossing a river with his boots on. But when Billy was on the prod, or happy, for that matter, he seemed as big as life. He was always smiling and flashing those pearly white teeth. One look at him and you knew it was all fun, and damn the consequences.

Andy had pretty white teeth, except for the two front ones that were missing. He said a calf had kicked them out. I rose and started to hang my blankets to dry on the log.

"No time for that," Billy said. "That's Commission Creek, and she heads up not too far from here. We should be able to cross, as she's falling fast and is pretty narrow and shallow on up there."

"My horse might not carry this wet bedroll." Sleeping in a hurricane never made me what you could call chipper in the morning.

"That sore-footed driblet might not carry you out of camp." Billy pointed to my new horse.

"What the hell is a driblet?"

"You know, a driblet." There was the faint trace of a smirk at the corner of Billy's mouth. He was enjoying my ignorance of his newfound vocabulary.

"No, I don't know what a driblet is. I think you're making it up." I wasn't about to be buffaloed.

Billy walked a wide semicircle around my horse, making a big show of judging the quality of him. "Yep, that's what I thought. He fits the bill."

I waited for him to continue, not about to bite the bait he was laying out for me. Billy hacked up a little wad in his throat and let the ball hang for a minute from his lip until it fell slowly to the ground.

"That's a driblet. It ain't quite spit, and it ain't quite drool. It's a driblet." Billy jabbed a thumb at my little horse, who stood three-legged under the cottonwoods with his nose practically on the ground and his bottom lip sagging. He might have weighed seven hundred pounds saddled. "That's a driblet."

Andy snorted and whistled through the hole in his teeth. "You beat all, Billy."

"Maybe the sun will pop out later and we can stop and dry our gear." I was annoyed at Andy for no reason. But then again, I was generally annoyed at Andy most of the time.

"I'll go bring up the horses if I can, and catch 'Horsekiller' here a mount." I was perfectly willing to leave so as not to give Billy the chance to gloat.

I was just about out of earshot when I heard Andy whine, "Catch me a good'un, Nate!"

Like there was a good one in the bunch. It was a pretty sorry-looking herd of horses, and only three outlaw cowboys would be stupid enough to risk life and limb stealing them. Much as those Cheyenne liked to race, you would have thought they would ride better horses. Maybe that's why they hadn't caught us, because it just wasn't worth the effort. They proba-bly gave up chasing us as soon as they had put on a little show of trying to shoot and scream us into the hereafter.

That might have been the case, but I wasn't taking any chances. I would keep a watch over my shoulder all the way to

Kansas. When they were burning rifle friction over our heads I took them plumb serious. We were lucky to have outrun them, but Billy had figured it that way. It was early spring, the grass just starting to green up, and he claimed that if we rode horses that had wintered with a little corn, we could outrun any pursuit by Cheyenne on winter-starved ponies.

To my own way of figuring, I thought that the Cheyenne didn't have a good horse left among them, what with every cowboy wintering in the Cherokee Strip to the north driving them off, and with the soldiers around the reservation keeping the bucks from stealing any new replacements.

The horses weren't scattered too far at all because they were mostly gutted and worn out. I roped a little bay that looked in better flesh than most of the others. Billy joined me on the paint. As he swung around to the other side of them, I laughed as the paint repeatedly boogered, jumping sideways every so often as he kept looking back at Billy on his back. That served Billy right for being foolish enough to ride him. Nobody in those days wanted to ride a paint horse.

We started the ponies up the creek. They were moving slowly, without any travel to them. I left them to Billy and led the bay to Andy. It was a five-minute ordeal saddling him, but Andy finally got a leg tied up and got it done.

"Wish I had my hat. My head don't feel right," he complained.

"I wish you had a lick of sense. Slip his foot loose and let's go."

Andy pulled loose the slipknot holding up the near hind foot and hung his rope from his saddle horn. Gathering up his reins, he carefully stepped aboard. The bay tensed and humped up like a cat with a watermelon on his back. "He don't act sociable, do he?"

The bay stood stock-still and trembling until Andy let out his version of a Comanche war whoop and tapped both rowels into that pony's blown-up belly. Bay shot straight up and landed, all fours bunched up and too cinchy to move. Andy motivated him again, and they lit out up the creek. The bay bawled and stiff-legged all the way. Say what you wanted to about Andy, but the kid could sit a bucking horse.

The sorrel I rode had been ridden a little before, but he was a far cry from broke. His feet were too sore to give me much trouble, and I contented myself to amble along back to Billy. Andy came by me, his horse still crow-hopping a little ways and then stopping. Andy would spank him out of it, and they would go a little ways and repeat the process.

"I don't think this boy's been rode before. How am I supposed to herd horses?" Andy said as he plunged past me.

"Keep his nose pointed the way you want to go. Kick when you need to move, and pull when you want to stop," I advised.

"I hear you."

I'd never done anything but cowboy since I was big enough to count for anything. It seemed like that was a hand's job in those days. You were expected to herd wild cattle on the back of a horse just as wild. I have seen and ridden some good animals, broke to death, gentle, the kind you could do something on. There were good cutting horses worth a fortune beyond me, and good roping horses that you weren't afraid to tie to and rope just about anything. Every hand had one to tell about, but most of the time you were riding some sorry bronc that would as soon stomp you as look at you.

We caught up to Billy. He put a lead on the herd, and Andy and I brought them along, pushing up on the drag until we broke them into a good long trot. We were quite the sight, all of us on green or unbroken horses. Andy's horse continued to pitch, and Billy's paint shied at everything from Billy to a clump of grass that didn't look right. Hell, I even saw it fart and spook itself. There was something about the splashy-colored devil that had outlaw written all over him. I thought Billy was making a fool of himself over that nag. A knotheaded horse has been the misery of many a man, but if I'd known half the trouble that little paint horse was going to get us into, I'd have shot him on the spot.

We made our way upstream, waded across the creek, and rounded a little rock pile, a government survey marker that was the Texas line. Both Andy and Billy let out a whoop and kicked their horses up. Andy went so far as to turn a little circle at a lope, whooping and slapping his chaps leg in time as the bay broke into pitching again.

Crossing that little line must have meant a lot to those boys. The country in front of us looked just the same to me as what we had left behind, but then again, I wasn't from Texas. You would have thought those two were born in heaven and had just come home after fifty years in hell.

I knew better than to say anything or I would have to hear Billy expound upon the virtues of Texas for an hour. To my mind, that country might not even have been Texas, except by the say-so of Texans. There was nothing civilized that far north that I knew of, and damned sure no towns north of Mobeetie and east of Tascosa. But then again, those Texans would have claimed California and part of Canada as Texas ground if the world would let them.

Maybe we all carry a touch of the old home with us, packed away in its own little cubbyhole. They say home is where the heart is, but I was a restless, traveling sort of man. Those gusting winds drifted my wandering horse back and forth across the plains of endless grass until I was an orphan by my own choosing. I'll always remember home, not as a quaint picture of the place where I was born, but as a feeling. It was a rhythm of one hoof after another cutting prairie ground.

3

Swinging west of a little stage station, our stomachs be damned, we lined out north across a rolling, short-grass country scattered with gyp-rock canyons here and there. About noon we topped a hill and could see a long, flat descent down to a little creek cutting across our way. A small trickle of smoke drifted up from a camp below. I could make out what looked to be a cart with a couple of horses tied alongside.

Billy came loping back down the line and pulled up beside me. "What do you think?"

"My stomach thinks my throat's been cut."

Without another word, he lit out back to the front of the herd. We headed on down to the creek, the camp still some mile or so off. A hundred yards out, the horses in the camp nickered, and a few of ours answered. A sawed-off, bearded man with a Muley Sharps rifle in his hand came up to lean against the wheel of his cart.

Leaving the herd to scatter on grass, the three of us rode up and stopped about ten yards out from the fire. Billy spoke for us. "Howdy."

"Hi," the man beside the cart replied.

"We're driving north to Kansas and are all but out of grub. We wondered if you might have a bit to spare."

"I might." The whiskered gent looked us over for a bit and then strode to the fire. "Light and set."

All three of us ground-tied our mounts and then stepped up to the fire where the fellow had a pot of beans simmering. And I'll be danged if he didn't have a little batch of sourdough biscuits warming there. He dug out some plates from a kit in back of the cart, and we went at that food like a starving bitch wolf with pups. There wasn't enough silverware to go around. I came up short, but just raked mine off the plate with my knife straight into my mouth.

I slowed down long enough between bites on my second plate to study the wizened fellow across the fire from us. He sat Indian-fashion on the ground with that Sharps nestled across his thighs. He still eyed us suspiciously, or maybe there was a crafty look about him. He was extremely short, with an old, slouchy hat that hung down almost to the bridge of his nose. His gray beard draped over his potbelly. He might have been sixty, but his round little eyes were bright and sharp.

I noticed Billy was watching him just as closely as I was. I noticed too, that he was especially eyeing that Sharps-Borchardt rifle on the old man's lap. It looked to be brand spanking new. Depending on who you asked, cowboys had taken to calling that model a Muley Sharps either because it kicked like a mule or because it was a hammerless design and muley cattle were those without horns.

Now, I carried only a pistol, but Billy carried a Winchester too. He was always armed like a bandit. He claimed he carried a long gun for shooting meat and to keep some disagreements at a distance. He had a love for firearms, and that Muley Sharps had caught his eye.

"You boys taking those horses to Dodge?" Whiskers asked.

"Probably, or wherever we can find a buyer," Billy answered.

Now, even at a distance a person could see those horses for what they were. Up close, not more than four or five wore so much as a single brand. I could tell Whiskers was a trader, and he was eyeing that herd like Billy was eyeing that Sharps.

"I'm Billy Champion, this gent here to my right is Nate Reynolds, and the skinny galoot to my left is Andy."

"Andy Custer," Andy threw in. He insisted telling everyone he was kin to the late general.

Billy gave him an impatient look and continued, "If you've got a bit to spare, we could use a little grub to get us on through. We ain't got much hard money, but maybe we could deal you out of bit of salt and beans."

Whiskers didn't answer about the food. He looked past us out to where our horses grazed. "I heard of you. You're the man who backed John Jay down. Do you know you're on his range right now?"

Billy ignored the question just like Whiskers had done. Everyone in southwest Kansas, the western half of the Indian Territory, and probably back down the trail south into old Texas knew about Billy's run-in with Jay.

Jay's outfit took in a big chunk of country and was running a lot of cattle. Billy had brought a herd up from South Texas a year ago and delivered it to Jay's headquarters in Kansas. That's how Billy and I had met; I worked under him on that drive.

Billy and Jay disagreed on the delivery count, and things got a little heated. Like a lot of self-made men, John Jay thought a lot of himself, and he was used to running roughshod over lesser men. He cussed Billy for losing too many steers on the trail, cussed about their condition, and generally let Billy know what he thought about his poor abilities in regard to managing a trail herd. The recount on a hot day had clipped everyone's fuses pretty short. Before Jay had gotten good and wound up,

Billy put his hand on his Colt and told him they could settle things between them real quick if he had the guts. Jay backed down in front of our crew, and his. He paid up according to Billy's count, and the taste of humble pie didn't set too good with either him or his hands. He ought to have counted himself lucky that Billy didn't kill him right then. In those days, nobody would have denied Jay deserved anything he got. You had best be careful how you spoke to prideful men with pistols on.

I was just damned glad it didn't end up in a killing that day. It probably would have gotten both crews into it.

"Lot of trouble, driving horses," Whiskers said.

"What trouble?" Billy answered.

"The market can be doubtful, and it can take time to find a buyer."

"That's a good set of horses, and we've got time."

"It'll be tough to sell them in their winter clothes."

"The grass is greening; they're putting on weight as we speak. They'll be fat and summer-slick in a couple of weeks."

"It's hard to see them from here."

"I don't guess I'd mind showing them to you."

Two traders had met. Whiskers went behind the cart and untied a horse from the off-wheel. Billy rose and eased out to the paint. I mean he *eased*. The horse raised his head and snorted and made two bounds away from Billy before he managed to con his way up to him and get a hold.

"Little wild, ain't he?" Whiskers said as he rode up.

Billy stepped aboard. "He's a little green, but he's a traveler."

He reached down to rub the horse affectionately on the neck, and that paint traveled about twenty feet sideways in one jump. Whiskers cackled like an old hen, and the two of them made off for the herd.

Never one to pass on a chance to nap, Andy sprawled out in the grass. Me, I took the opportunity to study that peculiar little layout. The cart was not of the Mexican type, but rather a spoke-wheeled job with a single seat and a tarp on the bed. A one-eyed brown mare stood hip-shot alongside. She was galled with harness sores and so skinny you could almost see through her. The cart was a one-horse rig, and it was amazing to assume that she was responsible for pulling it.

The sun was busting through the clouds and hitting the ground, promising for a pretty day. Andy must have been enjoying it because he brought out the band, snoring to a tune all his own.

I took up a piece of sourdough and wiped the last of the bean juice from my plate. I watched Billy and Whiskers in the distance. They were drifting lazily through the grazing horses, stopping to study this one and that one from time to time. I knew the haggling was getting serious when at one stop I heard, even at a distance, Whiskers go to cussing until he gagged on his tobacco.

After what must have been half an hour, I decided to leave the bean pot and join the fun. As I rode up Billy motioned me on over to him.

"Put Driblet through his paces so this man can see I've told him correct."

Paces? Billy sat there smugly with a twinkle in his eye, like he expected me to have something to show him. With a sigh of surrender, I rode out from the herd and put on a little demonstration of what that sorrel nag couldn't do.

I pedaled him up to a lope with a good dose of my guthooks, and with a little finesse, managed to ride him in a big circle to the left. He was so sore-footed it was a job to keep him from breaking stride, and he had a trot that would jar the front teeth out of a beaver. He wrung his tail in frustration and jacked up his head and gaped his mouth against the bit. I pulled him down slowly to what you could call a stop, made an attempt to roll him back the other way, and loped a couple of circles to the right. I headed back to the horse traders, not aiming directly at them, as I wasn't sure I could stop short enough to keep from crashing into their midst. I took a severe hold and bit-bumped him into the ground.

Whiskers grunted his approval and spat tobacco juice out in a thick black arc. "Stops hard, don't he?"

I didn't want to tell him just how hard it was.

"Just like I told you, he can turn around like a cat in a stovepipe, stop on a dime, and get back like a bad check," Billy chimed.

"Smooth, ain't he," Whiskers added.

I was beginning to get a good handle on his horse appraisal skills. "I'd say so."

"See there, and he's pretty to boot," Billy said.

The sorrel did have a flaxen mane and tail, a big blaze face, and two socks on his hind feet. Beyond that, you couldn't tell where the ugly stopped and the horse began. He was so narrow you couldn't have passed your fist between his front legs, and he had a long, thin bottle head that was disproportionately large in comparison to the rest of his body.

The horses were drifting farther down the creek looking for grass, and I left to go bring them back a little closer to camp. When I returned, Billy left Whiskers and rode up to me for a private discussion of the kind that happens when parties are horse-trading.

"You know, we might get ten to twelve dollars a head for those horses in Kansas *if* we found a buyer. And those soldiers down south may have got word we stole them and wired the news north. It's happened before," Billy said solemnly. "If we could make a good trade here, it'd be better than going to some farmer's calaboose over a bunch of ten-dollar Cheyenne ponies."

"What's the trade?"

"Five dollars a head, and we take the cut with us, or throw them in."

"Cash money?"

"Well, that's a lot of hard money. Let's see"—Billy made a show of tabulating on his fingers—"fifty head minus one that's got a knocked-down hip, one with an eye put out, and five that a coyote wouldn't eat. Let's say ten head of cuts. That's forty head at five dollars." He fired up his finger adding machine again.

"Two hundred," I said impatiently.

"Yeah, two hundred. How's that sound?"

"Hard money?"

"Well . . ."

"How much hard money?" I could see where things were headed.

Billy tried one of his smiles to frame the wonderful price he was fixing to shoot at me. "Sixty-five cash, that Sharps gun, fifty rounds of friction for it, and a little sack of victuals."

"Who gets the gun?"

"You can have my old Winchester."

"What about Andy?" We sometimes forgot about Andy, and I felt it my job to see that he was treated in a Christian fashion.

"I've got an old converted Colt Navy in my bedroll that he's been wanting. I'll give it to him so we all get a new shooting iron. We'll split the cash three ways."

"That old Navy ain't worth ten dollars."

"Once I tell Andy that Wild Bill Hickok favored Navy Colts, he'll think he's getting a hell of a deal. He'll probably become a two-gun badass himself," Billy snorted. "Besides, the boy's gotta pay something for the education we've been giving him."

"That'll work." I agreed readily, satisfied that things were divided equally enough.

"Just think, partner. We can drift down to Mobeetie and have a sure enough good time with that money." He slapped his thigh in sheer exuberance.

Billy felt it was his job to always keep my spirits up. After two years of riding with him I'd come to learn how to get at the truth of things when he told me something. When Billy was trying to convince you to go along with what he suggested, whether good news or bad, you just had to divide everything by two. Things were just generally halfway like he said they were. If he told you about a trip and you didn't want to go, he would tell you it was only a two-day ride. It would wind up taking four. If he told about a hundred dollars to be made at something and you went along, you might make fifty. He wasn't a liar; he just got too enthused with convincing you to go along with his plans.

"You can have my saddle horse," Billy said.

"What are you going to ride?" I was shocked by Billy's generous mood.

"I'm keeping the paint."

I threw a disgusted look at the paint and headed out to rope Billy's horse out of the herd. I'd lost my personal saddle horse somewhere in our flight with the stolen herd and was more than happy to take Dunny. He was as gentle and dependable as the day was long. Billy could have that flashy little pinto nag if he wanted him. He probably thought the horse matched his ivory-handled pistol.

"Who's going to help Whiskers drive that bunch?" I asked.

"That fellow looking over the creek bank pointing a shotgun at us," Billy burst out, obviously enjoying my shock and growing discomfort.

Sure enough, after he pointed out the direction I could make out somebody looking at us over a cutbank in the creek. He had been there all along, not ninety feet from us when we were at the fire. That would have made most folks nervous.

"Old Whiskers ain't too trusting," I said.

"His name is Harvey."

"I'll call him some other things once we get out of here. I don't like anybody pointing a gun at me, especially when I don't know they're there."

We rode back to Harvey Whiskers's camp, and Billy was smiling like somebody holding a gun on him was the funniest thing in the world. I threw my saddle on Dunny, proud to have the little black dun, what a lot of folks call a line-backed buckskin.

Harvey began pulling his saddle from the horse he was riding. "I think I might keep that sorrel for my own personal horse."

"I bet you'll love him," I replied.

I stepped up on Dunny, and Billy came up with a little canvas sack of grub that he handed up to me.

"Get up, Andy," Billy hollered.

Andy didn't stir until I walked Dunny over the top of him. He sprang from the grass in one move. "That horse could have stepped on me!"

"Mount up."

While Andy went out to get his horse, Billy handed me his Winchester and shoved the Sharps in his own saddle boot. I took a latigo string from a bunch I carried on my back dee and tied it to the saddle ring on the carbine. As soon as I'd hung it on my saddle horn, Harvey walked up and paid us the currency. Billy held the coins out in his palm to eye them appreciatively. Reaching down, I snatched a twenty-dollar gold piece and a few dollars more from the little pile in his hand and pocketed them.

"Hey! We've gotta divide it evenly!" Billy cried.

"If you were an educated man you'd call that an eyeball-cut." I laughed and started to turn away.

Harvey was saddling the sorrel, and he called out across the horse's back, "I'd say that wasn't much of an accurate split."

"I'd say you'd better call in that man you got out yonder. I'm tired of my back feeling most too wide." I wasn't feeling funny anymore.

I wasn't about to try to ride out of there with Whiskers's money only to give it back to him after I was shot in the back. Common sense and experience made me wary, and with Billy along I would have thought nothing of bearding the Devil in his den.

Harvey didn't argue any and waved his man on in. A big black fellow came walking up out of the creek with a long-barreled shotgun cradled in one huge elbow. That man was a giant and must have stood halfway past six feet. One of his legs was as big around as my chest. He wore a big-brimmed straw sombrero, a rough calico cloth shirt, and a pair of patched overalls that ended about three-quarters of the way down his calves.

"You want me to hitch up the mare, Mister Harvey?" The man's voice was deep and slow.

Andy rode up just as that fellow spoke, and I thought he'd break a spring. "Where the hell did he come from?"

"Let's go." Billy reached up and tucked some of the money into Andy's vest pocket.

Andy wasn't having any of it. His voice raised a notch higher. "Has that nigger been holding a gun on us all this time?"

I studied the black man standing there like a tree. He was as calm as can be, with that shotgun looking awfully little on his arm. A quiet man can be the one to watch in a fight, and despite his outward calm, I could tell he would scrap at the drop of a hat if Andy continued to push him.

"Let's go, Andy." I tried to relate the seriousness of the situation in my voice.

"That nigger don't scare me none," Andy sneered.

That black man's face might as well have been chiseled from

stone, but I noticed his thumb ease up onto the hammer of his scattergun. I figured I'd have to shoot him, but by then it would probably be too late for Andy. That shotgun had two holes in the end of it big enough to stick your thumbs in. A double-barrel ten-gauge with full chokes at fifty feet can be a serious proposition. A man might miss, even with a shotgun, but who in their right minds would want to chance it?

Before things got too Western, Billy shoved his horse against Andy's. "Let's go."

Andy didn't want to leave without a fight, but Billy spurred into him, and Andy's horse staggered, turning away from camp in order to regain its balance. Before he could turn back, Billy cut Andy's horse across the rump with his hat. That bay horse farted, gathered them up, and took off in a runaway with Andy hauling back on his mouth to no avail.

Billy eyed the black man for a long moment. A second seems like an awful long time in a situation like that. Billy could be a little abrupt when it came to disagreements, and I resigned myself to whatever was about to happen.

"Was there enough grub in that sack to suit you?" Harvey's voice interrupted the staring match.

Harvey must have had more sense than I had thought to change the subject. Of course, there would come a time when I would rethink a lot of the things about people I had judged in my past, some of them sooner rather than later.

"It'll do," Billy said to Harvey, but he was still looking at the black man.

Billy wasn't one to pick a fight, but I knew he wouldn't let anybody think they had run him off. We had been in the act of leaving when Harvey called up his man, but that didn't keep Billy from taking the time to roll a cigarette and study the weather for a bit. That black man hadn't said a word to us or threatened with his gun. Still, the calm, massive presence of him challenged us, and Billy seemed to feel it most.

"I wonder if Andy has gotten his horse stopped yet?" Billy finally asked me.

He turned the paint and we took our own sweet time riding away from camp, as if there wasn't a gun at our backs. Andy was long gone, obviously unable to turn his cold-jawed pony. Once we reached the crest of a big hill we struck a lope to catch up to him, and I turned in the saddle for one more look back. Harvey had gone to saddling the sorrel we had sold him, but that black man stood in the same spot like he was rooted there. He appeared determined to watch us until we were out of sight.

About half a mile over the hill, Andy loped back to meet us. "You'd no call to do that, Billy. No nigger ever backed me down."

Andy was just about as mad at Billy as he was at that black man. However, he worshipped Billy too much to want to shoot him—or kill him anyway. While the two of them jawed back and forth, I happened to look to our east. About two miles off I could see a long plume of dust worming its way toward Harvey's camp.

"You two look yonder. I think that's those Cheyenne fogging up our trail." I didn't wait for an answer. I just stuck the spurs to Dunny and headed west.

Billy and Andy didn't take long in following suit. We ran that way for about a mile and then hit some canyon country and slowed to a long trot. We stopped just off the edge of a big canyon, looking back the way we had come and listening for sounds of a fight. There were no gunshots, and the wind was blowing too hard to hear anything else.

"I wonder what that nigger thinks about a bunch of mad Cheyenne?" Andy was obviously pleased.

"I hope that old man is a talker," I said.

"I hope they gave him a chance to talk," Billy replied.

"He was a crafty sort, and if he does squirm his way out, those Cheyenne can read sign."

"You always look at the bright side, Nate." Billy shook his head at me.

"I'm still kicking, and I intend to be tomorrow."

I made sure to keep my eye on our back trail as we circled south. An old frontiersman once told me that the best way to stay in some semblance of good health in Indian country was to always keep your eyes upon the skyline and never sleep beside your fire. Maybe I was just a natural-born worrier, but I had no confidence in my luck or fate to favor me with fortune.

"I'm too busy having fun to worry." Nothing could faze Andy. "We'll have a time in Mobeetie come tomorrow, won't we, boys?"

"Hell yes, let's ride! There's whiskey, gambling, and a good-hearted whore waiting on me!" Billy hollered and raced off.

Both of them were soon riding beside each other, laughing about the time they were going to have and the trouble they might get into. Before long I was feeling it too, and my worries were slowly left behind along with what little good sense I had. Sometimes all a man needs to forget his cares is a little recreation and a dose of harmless misdemeanor. Yes sir, high times were coming to old Mobeetie. It was good sport, and damn the consequences when you rode with Billy Champion.

Index

198 / INDEX